The Tale of Helgi Thorisson

Original Text, Translations, and Word Lists

Translated by
Matthew Leigh Embleton

Copyright ©2025 Matthew Leigh Embleton. All rights reserved.

The Tale of Helgi Thorisson

The Tale of Helgi Thórisson (*Old Norse*)..4
Word List *(Old Norse to English)*..16
Word List *(English to Old Norse)* 25
The Tale of Helgi Thórisson (*Old Icelandic*) 32
Word List *(Old Icelandic to English)*...44
Word List *(English to Old Icelandic)*...53
A Word Comparison of Old Norse and Old Icelandic Words 60

Cover: Old Norse text over an outline of Iceland. Author's design.

The original Old Norse and Old Icelandic texts are in the public domain.
These translations ©2022 Matthew Leigh Embleton
©2025 Matthew Leigh Embleton (This Edition)

Acknowledgments

I have long been fascinated by languages and history, and I am very grateful to the special people in my life who have supported and encouraged me in my work. Thank you for believing in me. You know who you are.

Introduction

Old Norse is a North Germanic language spoken by inhabitants of Scandinavia from about the 7th to the 15th centuries. Old Icelandic is a variety of Old West Norse that emerged during the Norse settlement of Iceland in the second half of the 9th century. The rich tradition of Icelandic literature survived by oral tradition over several centuries before being written down in the 13th Century. The Tale of Helgi Þórisson (*Helga þáttr Þórissonar*) is one of the many Tales of Icelanders or *Íslendingaþættir*. The word '*þáttr*' (plural: '*þættir*') translates as a strand of rope or a yarn, comparable to the word 'yarn' in English sometimes used to refer to a story.

This book contains:
- The Tale of Helgi Þórisson (*Helga þáttr Þórissonar*) (Old Norse Version)
- An Old Norse to English Word List
- An English to Old Norse Word List
- The Tale of Helgi Þórisson (*Helga þáttr Þórissonar*) (Old Icelandic Version)
- An Old Icelandic to English Word List
- An English to Old Icelandic Word List
- A Word Comparison of Old Norse and Old Icelandic words

The texts are presented in their original form, with a literal word-for-word line-by-line translation, and a Modern English translation, all side-by-side. In this way, it is possible to see and feel how the worked and how it has evolved. This book is designed to be of use and interest to anyone with a passion for the Old Norse or Old Icelandic language, Norse history, or languages and history in general.

The Tale of Helgi Thórisson (*Old Norse*)

Old Norse	Literal	English
1	**1**	**1**
Þórir hét maðr, er bjó í Nóregi á bæ þeim, er á Rauðabergi heitir.	Thorir (name) was-named a-man, who settled in Norway (place) in a-farm that, was so Raudaberg (place) named.	There was a man named Thorir who lived in Norway on a farm that was named Raudaberg.
Þessi bær er skammt frá Víkinni.	This farm was short-distance from The-bay.	The farm was a short distance away from the bay.
Þórir átti tvá syni.	Thorir (name) had two sons.	Thorir had two sons.
Hét annarr Helgi, enn Þorsteinn annarr; báðir váru þeir þrifligir menn, ok var þó Helgi framar um íþróttir.	Was-named one Helgi (name), was Thorstein (name) another; both were they thriving men, and was though Helgi (name) above in sports.	One was named Helgi, the other was named Thorstein; they were both thriving men, though Helgi surpassed in sports.
Faðir þeira var hersir at nafnbót.	Father theirs was a-local-chief of rank.	Their father was a local chief of high rank.
Hann var í vináttu vit Óláf konung.	He was in friendship with Olaf (name) the-king.	He was friends with King Olaf.
Þat var á einu sumri, at þeir bræðr höfðu kaupferð norðr til Finnmerkr ok höfðu smjör ok flesk til kaups vit Finna.	It was in one summer, that the brothers had trading-voyage north to Finnmark (place) and had butter and bacon to trade with Sámi (name).	It was one summer, that the brothers had a trading voyage north to Finnmark, and they had butter and bacon to trade with the Sámi people.
Fengu þeir góða kaupferð ok heldu aptr at áliðnu sumri ok kómu um dag vit nes þat, er hét Vímund.	Got they good trade and busy returned in late summer and came about a-day to headland that, was named Vimund (name).	They had a good and busy trade and returned late in the summer and came about one day to a headland that was named Vimund.
Þar var allgóðr skógr.	There were all-good forests.	There were all-good woods.
Gengu þeir á land upp ok fengu nokkurt mösurtré.	Went they to land up and got some maple-tree.	They went up to the land and got some maple trees.
Verðr Helga lengra gengit í skóginn enn öðrum mönnum.	Became Helgi (name) longer going in the-forest than other people.	Helgi went further into the woods than the other people.

The Tale of Helgi Thórisson (Old Norse)

Old Norse	Literal	English
Síðan kastar yfir myrkri miklu, svá at hann hittir ekki til skipsins á þeim aptni; tekr nú ok skjótt at dimma af nótt.	Then cast over darkness great, so that he found not to ship and then after; took now and quickly to darkness of night.	Then a great darkness cast over, so that he could not find the ship; and then afterwards the darkness of night took quickly.
Þá sér Helgi, hvar tólf konur ríða ór skóginum.	Then saw Helgi (name), were twelve women riding through the-forest.	Then Helgi saw that there were twelve women riding through the forest.
Þær váru allar á rauðum hestum ok í rauðum reiðklæðum.	They were all on red horses and in red riding-clothes.	They were all on red horses and in red riding-clothes.
Þær stigu af baki.	They stepped from horseback.	They stepped down from their horses.
Allr reiðingr hestanna þá glóaði vit gull.	All riding horses then shone with gold.	All the horses they were riding shone with gold.
Ein bar þar af öllum um vænleik, ok allar aðrar þjóna henni, þessi inni sköruligu konu.	One surpassed there of all about beauty, and all others served her, this the bold-like woman.	One of them surpassed all the others in beauty, and all the others served this bold looking woman.
Hestar þeira gengu á gras.	Horses they went to graze.	The horses then went to graze.
Eptir þat settu þær niðr eitt fagrt tjald.	After that set they down one fair tent.	After that they set down a fair tent.
Var þat stafat með ýmsum litum ok víða gullskotit, ok öll höfuðin váru vit gull búin, er af upp gengu landtjaldinu, ok svá stöngin, er upp stóð, ok mikill gullknappr ofan á.	Was it staved with various colours and widely gold-laid, and all heads were with gold prepared, was of up going land-tent, and so the-pole, that up stood, and large golden-ball above it.	It was striped with various colours and widely laden with gold, and all the heads were prepared with gold, and so it was of this land tent, that all the poles that stood up had a large golden ball on top.
Ok er þær höfðu um búizt, reistu þær borð ok báru á margs konar krásir.	And when they had about prepared, raised they a-table and bore out many kinds-of food.	And when they had prepared all about, they raised a table and brought our many kinds of food.
Þá tóku þær handlaugar, vatnskarl ok munnlaugar, gervar af silfri, ok allt laugat í gulli.	Then took they hand-washing, basins and mouth-basins, fashioned of silver, and all bathed in gold.	They took to washing their hands, with basins and jugs, fashioned of silver, and all bathed in gold.

The Tale of Helgi Thórisson (Old Norse)

Old Norse	Literal	English
Helgi stóð nærri tjaldi þeira ok horfði á.	Helgi (name) stood near tent theirs and looked about.	Helgi stood near their tent and looked about.
Sú, er fyr þeim var, mælti:	So, was before them was, spoke:	The one who was in front of them spoke:
"Helgi, gakk hingat, ok þigg hér mat ok drykk með oss".	"Helgi (name), come here, and accept here food and drink with us".	"Helgi, come here, and accept food and drink with us".
Hann gerir svá.	He did so.	He did so.
Helgi sér, at þar er fríðr drykkr ok önnur fæðsla ok væn ker.	Helgi (name) saw, that there was beautiful drink and also feast and fair vessels.	Helgi saw that there were beautiful drinks and a feast with fair drinking vessels.
Þá váru borð ofan tekin ok hvílur búnar, ok váru þær miklu skrautligri enn annarra manna sængr.	Then were tables down taken and beds prepared, and were these much splendid than other peoples beds.	Then the tables were taken down and the beds were prepared, and these were much more splendid than other peoples' beds.
Sú kona spyrr Helga, er fyr þeim var, hvárt hann vilda heldr liggja einn saman eðr hjá henni.	So the-woman asked Helgi (name), that for them was, either he wished rather to-lay alone together or beside her.	The woman who was at the front asked Helgi if he wished to lay alone or beside her.
Helgi spyrr hana at nafni.	Helgi (name) asked her of name.	Helgi asked her name.
hon svarar:	she answered:	She answered:
"Ek heit Ingibjörg, dóttir Guðmundar af Glæsisvöllum".	"I am-named Ingibjorg (name), daughter Gudmund (name) of Glasir-Plains (place)".	"I am named Ingibjorg, daughter of Gudmund of Glasir Plains".
Helgi mælti:	Helgi (name) spoke:	Helgi spoke:
"Hjá þér vil ek liggja".	"Beside you wish I to-lay".	"I wish to lay beside you".
Ok svá gerðu þau þrjár nætr í samt.	And so did they three nights of together.	And so they did for three nights together.
Var þá bjart veðr; standa þau þá upp ok klæðast.	Was then bright weather; stood they then up and clothed.	When the weather was bright; they stood up and clothed.
Ingibjörg mælti þá:	Ingibjorg (name) spoke then:	Ingibjorg then spoke:

The Tale of Helgi Thórisson (Old Norse)

Old Norse	Literal	English
"Nú munum vit hér skilja.	"Now shall we here separate.	"Now we shall separate here.
Eru hér kistlar tveir, annarr er fullr af silfri, enn annarr af gulli, er ek vil gefa þér, ok seg engum manni, hvaðan þat kom".	There-are here chests two, one is full of silver, and another of gold, am I will to-give to-you, and say none person, from-where that came".	Here are two chests, one is full of silver, and another of gold, and I will give them to you, and you shall tell no person, where they came from".
Eptir þat ríða þær burt sama veg sem þangat, enn hann fór til skips síns.	After that rode they away the-same way as from-there, that he travelled to ships his.	After that they rode away the same way as they had come from, and he travelled to his ships.
Fagna þeir honum vel ok spyrja, hvar hann dvaldist, enn hann vill þar eigi frá segja.	Welcomed they him well and asked, where he dwelled, but he wished there not from to-say.	They welcomed him well and asked where he had stayed, but he did not wish to say.
Halda þeir þá suðr með landi ok koma heim til föður síns ok hafa aflat mikils fjár.	Held they then south along land and came home to father theirs and had surplus much wealth.	They held south along the land and came to their father's home and had much wealth.
Faðir Helga ok bróðir spyrja, hvaðan honum kom svá mikit fé sem hann hafði í kistlunum, enn hann vill þat ekki segja.	Father Helgi (name) and brother asked, from-where he came so much wealth as he had in chests, but he wished that not to-say.	Helgi's father and brother asked where he came by so much wealth as he had in his chests, but he did not wish to say.

2

Nú líðr svá fram til jóla.	Now passed so from until Yule.	Now it passed on to Yule.
Þat var eina nótt, at kemr á býsna veðr.	It was one night, that came an extreme weather.	And it was one night that there came extreme weather.
Þorsteinn mælti vit bróður sinn:	Thorstein (name) spoke with brother his:	Thorstein spoke with his brother:
"Vit skulum standa upp ok vita, hvat líðr um skip okkart".	"We should stand up and know, what passes about ship ours".	"We should get up and find out what is happening with our ship".
Þeir gera svá, ok var þat fast vel.	They did so, and was it fastened well.	They did so, and it was fastened well.

The Tale of Helgi Thórisson (Old Norse)

Old Norse	Literal	English
Helgi hafði látit gera drekahöfuð á skip þeira upp á stafnana ok búa vel fyr ofan sjó.	Helgi (name) had made done dragon's-head on ship theirs up in ship's-prow and prepared well for above the-sea.	Helgi had a dragon's head made for their ship's prow and it was decorated well above the sea level.
Fór þat fé þar til, er Ingibjörg gaf honum, dóttir Guðmundar konungs, enn sumt læsti hann í drekahálsinum.	Travelled the wealth there to, that Ingibjorg (name) gave him, daughter-of Gudmund (name) the-king, but some locked he in the-dragon's-neck.	The wealth that Ingibjorg, daughter of King Gudmund, gave him had travelled there but some of it was locked in the dragon's neck.
Þá heyra þeir brest mikinn.	Then heard they a-crash great.	Then they heard a great crash.
Þar ríða at þeim tveir menn ok höfðu Helga í burt með sér.	There riders at them two men and had Helgi (name) to away with them.	Then two men rode towards them and took Helgi away with them.
Veit Þorsteinn eigi, hvat af honum verðr.	Knew Thorstein (name) not, what of him became.	Thorstein did not know what became of him.
Fellr þá veðrit skjótt.	Fell then weather away.	The weather then fell away.
Þorsteinn kemr heim ok segir föður sínum þenna atburð, ok þykkir þetta mikil tíðendi.	Thorstein (name) came home and told father his these events, and thought that much news.	Thorstein came home and told his father of these events, and thought that this news was very much.
Ferr hann þegar á fund Óláfs konungs ok segir honum, hvar komit var, ok biðr hann nú verða vissan um, hvar er sonr hans er niðr kominn.	Travelled he straight-away to meet Olaf (name) the-king and said to-him, what came was, and asked him now to-become knowledge about, where was son his and son become.	He travelled straight away to meet King Olaf and told him what had happened, and asked him for knowledge about where his son was and what had become of him.
Konungr segist þat gera mundu, sem hann beiddi, enn kveðst þó óvíst hugr um segja, hverr nyt frændum hans mynda at honum verða.	The-King said that do would, that-which he asked, but said though uncertain thought about said, any use kinsman he should to him become.	The king said that he would do what he asked, but said that it was uncertain to say, if his kinsman would be of any use after what had happened to him.
Síðan fór Þórir heim, ok líðr svá þetta ár ok allt fram á jól annat ár, ok sitr konungr á Alreksstöðum um vetrinn.	After travelled Thorir (name) home, and passed so that year and all from to Yule another year, and sat the-king in Alreksstead (place) about winter.	Afterwards Thorir travelled home, and so passed that year to Yule, and the king sat in Alrekstead over the winter.

The Tale of Helgi Thórisson (Old Norse)

Old Norse	Literal	English
Þá kemr átti dagr jóla, ok um kveldit ganga þrír menn í höllina fyr Óláf konung, þá er hann sat yfir borðum.	Then came eighth day Yule, and about evening went three men in the-hall before Olaf (name) the-king, then as he sat over the-table.	Then came the eighth day of Yule, and at about evening three men entered the hall before King Olaf, as he sat across the tables.
Þeir kveðja hann vel.	They greeted him well.	They greeted him well.
Konungr heilsar þeim vel í móti.	The-King greeted them well in return.	The king greeted them well in return.
Er þar kominn Helgi, enn menn kenna ekki hina tvá.	Then there came Helgi (name), but people knew not the two.	Then there came Helgi, but people did not know who the other two were.
Konungr spurði þá at nafni, enn hvárrtveggi kveðst Grímr heita.	The-King asked then the names, and each said Grim (name) was-named.	The king asked their names, and each said their name was Grim.
"Erum vit sendir af Guðmundi á Glæsisvöllum hingat til yðar.	"We-are with sent of Gudmund (name) of Glasir-Plains (place) here to you.	"We have been sent by Gudmund of Glasir Plaines here to you.
Hann sendi yðr kveðju sína ok þar með tvau horn".	He sends you greetings his and there as-well two horns".	He sends you greetings and here as well two horns".
Konungr tók við, ok váru gullbúin.	The-King received with, and was gold-inlaid.	The king received them, and they were inlaid with gold.
Þetta váru allgóðir gripir.	They were all-gold treasures.	They were all good treasures.
Óláfr konungr átti tvau horn, er Hyrningar váru kallaðir, ok þó at þau væra harðla góð, þá váru þau þó betri, er Guðmundr sendi honum.	Olaf (name) the-king had two horns, were Hyrnings (name) were called, and though that they were greatly good, then were they though better, that Gudmund (name) sent him.	King Olaf had two horns, that were called Hyrnings, and though they were great, the ones that Gudmund had sent him were better.
"Þess beiddi Guðmundr konungr yðr, herra, at þér værið vinir hans, ok þótti mestu varða um yðra þykkju, meir enn allra annarra konunga".	"This bids Gudmund (name) the-king to-you, lord, that to-you become friend his, and thinks most warrant about yours things, more than all other kings".	"This Gudmund asks you, lord, that you become his friend, as he values you as more important than all other kings".
Konungr segir þá engu, enn lætr vísa þeim til sætis félögum.	The-King answered then not, but had directed them to seats company.	The king did not answer then, but directed them to the seats with company.

The Tale of Helgi Thórisson (Old Norse)

Old Norse	Literal	English
Konungr lætr fylla hornin Gríma af góðum drykk ok lætr byskup blessa ok lét færa þeim Grímum, at þeir drykki fyrst af.	The-King had filled the-horns Grim (name) of good drink and had bishop bless and had brought them Grims (name), that they drank first of.	The king had the Grim horns filled of good drink and had a bishop bless them and bring them to the Grims, so that they drank first.
Þá kvað konungr vísu þessa:	Then spoke the-king a-verse this:	Then the king spoke this verse:
"Gestir skulu hornum í gegn taka, meðan hvílast látum þenna þegn Guðmundar, ok af samnafna sínum drekki; svá skal Grímum gott öl gefast".	"The-guests shall horns to directly take, while rest have they thane Gudmund (name), and of same-name theirs drink; so shall Grims (name) good ale give".	The guests shall these horns directly take, while they have rest thane of Gudmund, of his namesake theirs drink; so shall the Grims give good ale".
Þá taka Grímar vit hornunum ok þykkjast nú vita, hvat byskup hefir yfir lesit drykkinum.	Then took Grims (name) with the-horns and realised now certainly, what the-bishop had over read drinks.	Then the Grims took the horns and realised now with certainty, what the bishop had read over these drinks.
Þeir segja þá:	They said then:	They then said:
"Eigi ferr nú fjarri því, sem Guðmundr, konungr várr, gat til.	"Not travel now far-away because, as Gudmund (name), the-king ours, could to.	"Now do not go far from what Gudmund, our king, could do.
Er þessi konungr prettóttr ok kann illa gott at launa, því at konungr várr gerði til hans sæmiliga.	Is this king deceitful and can evil good to repay, therefore the king aware be to him well-enough.	This king is deceitful and repays good with evil, therefore the king should be well enough aware.
Stöndum nú upp allir ok verðum í brottu heðan".	Stand now up all and have to away hence".	Let's get up and go right now".
Svá gera þeir.	So did they.	They did so.
Verðr þá hark mikit í stofunni.	Became then noise much in the-room.	Then there was much noise in the room.
Þeir slógu niðr drykkinum af hornunum ok slökktu login.	They threw down the-drinks of the-horns and put-out lights.	The threw down the drinks from the horns and put out the lights.
Þá heyrðu þeir bresti stóra.	Then heard they crash great.	Then they heard a great crash.

The Tale of Helgi Thórisson (Old Norse)

Old Norse	Literal	English
Konungr bað guði til gæta ok bað menn upp standa ok stöðva þetta hark.	The-King prayed God to guard and bid men up stand and stop this racket.	The king prayed to God to guard him and asked his men to stand up and stop this racket.
Síðan verða þeir Grímar úti ok Helgi með þeim.	Afterwards were they The-Grims (name) outside and Helgi (name) with them.	Afterwards the Grims were outside and Helgi was with them.
Váru þá ljós upp tendruð í konungs herbergi.	Were then lights up lit in the-king's room.	Then the lights were lit up in the king's room.
Sjá þeir þá drepna þrjá menn, enn þar liggja hornin Grímar á gólfinu hjá inum dauðum.	Saw they then killed three men, and there laid horns The-Grims' (name) by the-floor beside the dead.	They then saw that three men had been killed, and the Grims' horns were on the floor beside the dead.
"Þetta er undr mikit", sagði konungr, "ok væra betr, at slík yrði sjaldan.	"This is strange much", said the-king, "and should-be better, that such becomes seldom.	"This is very strange", said the king, "and it would be best if this becomes seldom.
Ok þat hef ek heyrt sagt af Guðmundi af Glæsisvöllum, at hann sé mjök fjölkunnigr ok illu megi helzt vit hann skipta, ok eru þeir menn illa komnir, er undir hans valdi eru, ef vér mættum nokkut at gera".	And that have I heard said of Gudmund (name) of Glasir-Plains (place), that he is a-great skilled-in-magic and evil may keep with him divide, and they-are the people evil comes, who under his control are, if we may anything to do".	And I have heard said of Gudmund of Glasir Plains, that he is greatly skilled in magic and his evil keeps dividing, and the people under his control are evil, even if anything may be done about it".
Konungr lét varðveita hornin Gríma ok af drekka, ok dugir þat vel.	The-king had preserved the-horns Grims' (name) and of drank, and enough it-was well.	The king had the Grim horns preserved and drank from them, and all was well enough.
Þar er nú kallat Grímaskarð ofan at Alreksstöðum, er þeir hafa austan farit, ok er þat engra manna at fara þar síðan.	There is now called Grim-Pass (place) over at Alreksstead (place), where they had east travelled, and is that no people to travel there since.	There is a mountain pass called Grim Pass over at Alreksstead where they travelled east, and no people have travelled there since.

3

Nú líðr af vetrinn, ok kemr annarr átti dagr jóla, ok er konungr í kirkju ok hirð hans at hlýða messu.	Now passed of winter, and came another eighth day Yule, and was the-king in church and retainers his at attending mass.	Now it passed to winter, and another eighth day of Yule, and the king was in church with his retainers attending mass.

The Tale of Helgi Thórisson (Old Norse)

Old Norse	Literal	English
Þá koma þar þrír menn til kirkjudyra, ok er einn eptir, enn tveir fara í brott ok mæla þetta áðr:	Then came there three men to church-door, and was one after, but two travelled to away and spoke this before:	Then there came three men to the church door, one of they stayed behind, but two travelled away and said before they went:
"Hér færum vit þér Gretti, konungr, ok er ekki víst, nær þú færir af þér".	"Here travelled with to-you Gretti (name), king, and that not certain, when you bring out-of you-to".	"Here we bring to you Gretti, king, and it is not certain how you will be able to get rid of him".
Kenna menn þar Helga.	Knew people there Helga (name).	People came to know that it was Helgi.
Síðan gengr konungr til borða, ok er menn tala vit Helga, verða menn þess varir, at hann er blindr.	Afterwards went the-king to the-table, and as people spoke with Helga (name), became people this aware, that he was blind.	Afterwards the king went to the tables, and as people spoke with Helgi, the became aware, that he was blind.
Frétti konungr þá, hverju gegndi um hans hag eðr hvar hann hefði verit þessa stund alla.	Inquired the-king then, each reason about his circumstances and where he had been this time all.	The king then inquired about each of the reasons of his circumstances and where he had been all this time.
Hann segir þá konungi fyrst frá því, er hann fann konurnar í skóginum, þá frá því, er þeir Grímar gerðu veðrit at þeim bræðrum, er þeir vildu bjarga skipinu, ok síðan höfðu þeir Grímar hann með sér til Guðmundar á Glæsisvöllum ok færðu hann Ingibjörgu, dóttur Guðmundar.	He told then the-king first from accordingly, and he found women in the-forest, then from accordingly, that they The-Grims (name) made a-storm that they the-brothers, and they wished to-save the-ship, and afterwards had they The-Grims (name) him along himself to Gudmund (name) of Glasir-Plains (place) and travelled he Ingibjorg (name), daughter-of Gudmund (name).	He told the king accordingly from the beginning, how he found the women in the forest, that the Grims who were brothers had made a storm come upon the brothers, and how they wishes to save their ship, and afterwards how they took him to Gudmund of Glasir Plains and delivered him to Ingibjorg, daughter of Gudmund.
Þá mælti konungr:	Then spoke the-king:	Then the king spoke:
"Hversu þótti þér þar at vera?"	"How-so thought you there to be?"	"How did you find it there?",
"Allgott", segir hann, "ok hverrgi hefir mér betra þótt".	"All-good", said he, "and nowhere have I better thought".	"All good", said he, "and nowhere have I thought better".
Þá spurði konungr at um siðu Guðmundar konungs ok at fjölmenni eðr athöfn.	Then asked the-king that about customs Gudmund (name) the-king and to followers or deeds.	Then the king asked about the customs of Gudmund and his followers and their deeds.

The Tale of Helgi Thórisson (Old Norse)

Old Norse	Literal	English
enn hann lét yfir öllu vel ok sagði, at hans var miklu fleiri enn hann fengi talit.	then he had over all well and said, that he was much more than he got counted.	Then he had said well about all, and that there was more than he could count to tell them.
Konungr mælti:	The-king spoke:	The king spoke:
"Hví fóru þér svá skjótliga í brott í fyrra vetr?"	"Why travelled you so shortly to away the first winter?"	"Why did you travel away so quickly the first winter?",
"Guðmundr konungr sendi þá til at svíkja yðr", segir hann, "en fyr bænir yðrar lét hann mik lausan, svá at þér mættið vita, hvat er af mér væra orðit.	"Gudmund (name) the-king sent them to of fool you", said he, "but for prayers yours had he me released, so that you may know, what was of me was become.	"King Gudmund sent them to fool you", he said, "but for your prayers he had me released, so that you may know what had become of me.
enn því fóru vér svá skjótt í brott næstunni, at þeir Grímar höfðu ekki náttúru til at drekka þann drykk, er þér létuð signa.	but because travelled we so shortly to away the-last-time, that they The-Grims (name) had not the-nature to of drink the drink, which you had signed.	But because we travelled so quickly away the last time, the Grims did not have the nature to drink the drink that you had signed.
Urðu þeir þessu reiðir, at þeir sá sik yfirstigna, ok því drápu þeir menn yðra, at svá sagði Guðmundr konungr fyrir, ef þeir fengi eigi mein yðr gert.	Became they this angry, that they saw themselves surpassed, and therefore killed they people yours, that so told Gudmund (name) the-king before, if they got not harm yours done.	They became angry that you had surpassed them, and therefore they killed your people, because King Gudmund told them to do so, if they could not do harm to you.
enn hann sýndi tign sína í því, at hann sendi yðr hornin, at þér mundið þá síðr eptir mér leita".	but he showed prestige his in because, that he sent you the-horns, that you remember then less afterwards me seeking".	But he showed his prestige in sending you the horns, so that you would remember less about seeking me".
Konungr spurði:	The-king asked:	The king asked:
"Hví fórtu nú í brott öðru sinni?"	"Why travelled now to away the-other with?"	"Why did you go away this time?",
Hann svarar:	He answered:	he answered:
"Ingibjörg olli því.	"Ingibjorg (name) caused therefore.	"Because of Ingibjorg.

The Tale of Helgi Thórisson (Old Norse)

Old Norse	Literal	English
hon þóttist ekki mega liggja hjá mér nema með meinlætum, ef hon kæmi vit mik beran, ok því fór ek mest í brott, enda vilda Guðmundr konungr eigi þreyta vit yðr, þegar hann vissi, at þér vilduð mik í brott hafa.	she thought not may lay beside me without with malignance, if she came with me bare, and because-of travelled I most to away, and wished Gudmund (name) the-king not tired with you, as-soon-as he knew, that you willed me to away at-sea.	She thought that she may no longer lay beside me without feeling uneasy whenever she came into contact with me bare, and for that reason most I travelled away, and King Gudmund did not wise to be tired of you, as soon as he knew that you willed me to go away to sea.
enn um tign ok risnu Guðmundar konungs má ek ekki í fám orðum segja ok um fjölmenni þat, er með honum er".	but about prestige and hospitality Gudmund (name) the-king may I only of few words to-say and about followers that, are with him are".	But about the prestige and hospitality of King Gudmund I have little words to say about it or the followers that are with him there".
Konungr spurði:	The-king asked:	The king asked:
"Hví ertu blindr?"	"Why are-you blind?"	"Why are you blind?"
Hann svarar:	He answered:	He answered:
"Ingibjörg Guðmundardóttir greip ór mér bæði augun, þá er vit skildum, ok sagði, at konur í Nóregi mundri mín skamma stund njóta".	"Ingibjorg (name) Daughter-of-Gudmund (name) gripped from me both eyes, then when we separated, and said, that women in Norway (place) would my short while enjoy".	"Ingibjorg, daughter of Gudmund, gripped both my eyes from me, and then when we separated, she said that women in Norway would enjoy my company for a short while".
Konungr sagði:	The-king said:	The king said:
"Makligr væra Guðmundr meingerða af mér fyr þau manndráp, er hann gerði, ef guði vilda þat vera láta".	"Properly would-be Gudmund (name) harmed of me for those murders, that he did, if God would that be allowed".	"Gudmund would be properly harmed by me for those murders that he did, if God would allow it".
Síðan var sent eptir Þóri, föður Helga, ok þakkaði hann honum vel, er sonr hans var aptr kominn ór trölla höndum.	Afterwards was sent after Thori (name), father Helga's (name), and thanked he him well, that son his was returned come from monsters hands.	Afterwards Helgi's father Thorri was sent for and he thanked him well that his son was returned from the hands of such monsters.
Ferr hann síðan heim, enn Helgi er eptir með konungi ok lifir til annarrar jafnlengdar.	Travelled he then home, but Helgi (name) was after with the-king and lived until another equal-length.	He then travelled home, but Helgi was thereafter with the king and lived another year.

The Tale of Helgi Thórisson (Old Norse)

Old Norse	Literal	English
enn konungr hefir hornin Gríma með sér, þá er hann fór síðasta sinn ór landi.	then the-king had the-horns Grims' (name) with him, then when he travelled last his out-of land.	Then the king had the Grim horns with him, when he travelled last out of the land.
enn þat segja menn, þá er Óláfr konungr hvarf af Orminum langa, at hyrfi ok hornin ok hafa engi maðr þau sét síðan.	is it said people, then that Olaf (name) the-king disappeared from Serpent long, that disappeared also the-horns and has no man them seen since.	It is said by people, that then King Olaf disappeared from The Long Serpent, and that the horns also disappeared and no man has seen them since.
Ok lýkr hér frá Grímum at segja.	And concludes here from The-Grims (name) to say.	And here concludes what may be said about the Grims.

Word List *(Old Norse to English)*

Old Norse	English

A, a

Old Norse	English
aðrar	others
af	from, of, out-of
aflat	surplus
alla	all
allar	all
allgóðir	all-gold
allgóðr	all-good
Allgott	all-good
allir	all
Allr	all
allra	all
allt	all
Alreksstöðum	Alreksstead (place)
annarr	another, one
annarra	other
annarrar	another
annat	another
aptni	after
aptr	returned
at	at, in, of, that, the, to
atburð	events
athöfn	deeds
augun	eyes
austan	east

Á, á

Old Norse	English
á	about, an, and, by, in, it, of, on, out, so, to
áðr	before
áliðnu	late
ár	year
átti	eighth, had

B, b

Old Norse	English
bað	bid, prayed
báðir	both
bæ	a-farm
bæði	both
bænir	prayers
bær	farm
baki	horseback
bar	surpassed
báru	bore
beiddi	asked, bids
beran	bare
betr	better
betra	better
betri	better
bið	asked
bjarga	to-save
bjart	bright
bjó	settled
blessa	bless
blindr	blind
borð	a-table, tables
borða	the-table
borðum	the-table
bræðr	brothers
bræðrum	the-brothers
brest	a-crash
bresti	crash
bróðir	brother
bróður	brother
brott	away
brottu	away
búa	prepared
búin	prepared
búizt	prepared
búnar	prepared
burt	away
byskup	bishop, the-bishop
býsna	extreme

D, d

Old Norse	English
dag	a-day
dagr	day
dauðum	dead

16

Word List (Old Norse to English)

Old Norse	English
dimma	darkness
dóttir	daughter, daughter-of
dóttur	daughter-of
drápu	killed
drekahálsinum	the-dragon's-neck
drekahöfuð	dragon's-head
drekka	drank, drink
drekki	drink
drepna	killed
drykk	drink
drykki	drank
drykkinum	drinks, the-drinks
drykkr	drink
dugir	enough
dvaldist	dwelled

E, e

Old Norse	English
eða	and, or
ef	if
eigi	not, only
Ein	one
eina	one
einn	alone, one
einu	one
eitt	one
Ek	I
ekki	not
en	and, but, is, than, that, then, was
enda	and
engi	no
engra	no
engu	not
engum	none
Eptir	after, afterwards
er	am, and, are, as, is, that, then, was, were, when, where, which, who
ertu	are-you
eru	are, there-are, they-are
Erum	we-are

F, f

Old Norse	English
Faðir	father
fæðsla	feast
færa	brought
færðu	travelled
færir	bring
færum	travelled
Fagna	welcomed
fagrt	fair
fám	few
fann	found
fara	travel, travelled
farit	travelled
fast	fastened
fé	wealth
Fellr	fell
félögum	company
fengi	got
Fengu	got
ferr	travel, travelled
Finna	Sámi (name)
Finnmerkr	Finnmark (place)
fjár	wealth
fjarri	far-away
fjölkunnigr	skilled-in-magic
fjölmenni	followers
fleiri	more
flesk	bacon
föður	father
fór	travelled
fórtu	travelled
fóru	travelled
frá	from
frændum	kinsman
fram	from, from
framar	above
Frétti	inquired
fríðr	beautiful
fullr	full
fund	meet
fylla	filled
fyrir	before, for
fyrra	first
fyrst	first

Word List (Old Norse to English)

Old Norse	English

G, g

Old Norse	English
gæta	guard
gaf	gave
gakk	come
ganga	went
gat	could
gefa	to-give
gefast	give
gegn	directly
gegndi	reason
gengit	going
gengr	went
gengu	going, went
gera	did, do, done
gerði	be, did
gerðu	did, made
gerir	did
gert	done
gervar	fashioned
Gestir	the-guests
Glæsisvöllum	Glasir-Plains (place)
glóaði	shone
góð	good
góða	good
góðum	good
gólfinu	the-floor
gott	good
gras	graze
greip	gripped
Gretti	Gretti (name)
Gríma	Grim (name), Grims' (name)
Grímar	Grims (name), the-Grims (name), the-Grims' (name)
Grímaskarð	Grim-Pass (place)
Grímr	Grim (name)
Grímum	Grims (name), the-Grims (name)
gripir	treasures
guð	God
Guðmundar	Gudmund (name)
Guðmundardóttir	daughter-of-Gudmund (name)
Guðmundi	Gudmund (name)
Guðmundr	Gudmund (name)
gull	gold
gullbúin	gold-inlaid
gulli	gold
gullknappr	golden-ball
gullskotit	gold-laid

H, h

Old Norse	English
hafa	at-sea, had
hafði	had
hafi	has
hag	circumstances
Halda	held
hana	her
handlaugar	hand-washing
Hann	he, him
hans	he, him, his
harðla	greatly
hark	noise, racket
heðan	hence
hef	have
hefði	had
hefir	had, have
heilsar	greeted
heim	home
heita	was-named
heiti	am-named
heitir	named
heldr	rather
heldu	busy
Helga	Helga's (name), Helgi (name)
Helgi	Helgi (name)
helzt	keep
henni	her
hér	here
herbergi	room
herra	lord
hersir	a-local-chief
hestanna	horses
Hestar	horses

Word List (Old Norse to English)

Old Norse	English
hestum	horses
hét	named, was-named
heyra	heard
heyrðu	heard
heyrt	heard
hina	the
hingat	here
hirð	retainers
hittir	found
hjá	beside
hlýða	attending
höfðu	had
höfuðin	heads
höllina	the-hall
höndum	hands
honum	he, him, to-him
horfði	looked
horn	horns
hornin	horns, the-horns
hornum	horns
hornunum	the-horns
hugr	thought
Hún	she
hvaðan	from-where
hvar	were, what, where
hvarf	disappeared
hvárrtveggi	each
hvárt	either
hvat	what
hver	any
hvergi	nowhere
hverju	each
Hversu	how-so
Hví	why
hvílast	rest
hvílur	beds
hyrfi	disappeared
Hyrningar	Hyrnings (name)

I, i

Old Norse	English
illa	evil
illu	evil
Ingibjörg	Ingibjorg (name)
Ingibjörgu	Ingibjorg (name)
inni	the
inum	the

Í, í

Old Norse	English
í	in, of, the, to
íþróttir	sports

J, j

Old Norse	English
jafnlengdar	equal-length
jól	Yule
jóla	Yule

K, k

Old Norse	English
kæmi	came
kallaðir	called
kallat	called
kann	can
kastar	cast
kaupferð	trade, trading-voyage
kaups	trade
kemr	came
kenna	knew
ker	vessels
kirkju	church
kirkjudyra	church-door
kistlar	chests
kistlunum	chests
klæðast	clothed
kom	came
koma	came
kominn	become, came, come
komit	came
komnir	comes
kómu	came
kona	the-woman
konar	kinds-of
konu	woman
konung	the-king
konunga	kings
konungi	the-king

Word List (Old Norse to English)

Old Norse	English
konungr	king, the-King
konungs	the-king, the-king's
konur	women
konurnar	women
krásir	food
kvað	spoke
kveðja	greeted
kveðju	greetings
kveðst	said
kveldit	evening

L, l

Old Norse	English
læsti	locked
lætr	had
land	land
landi	land
landtjaldinu	land-tent
langa	long
láta	allowed
látit	made
látum	have
laugat	bathed
launa	repay
lausan	released
leita	seeking
lengra	longer
lesit	read
lét	had
létuð	had
líðr	passed, passes
lifir	lived
liggja	laid, lay, to-lay
litum	colours
ljós	lights
login	lights
lýkr	concludes

M, m

Old Norse	English
má	may
maðr	a-man, man
mæla	spoke
mælti	spoke
mættið	may
mættum	may
Makligr	properly
manna	people, peoples
manndráp	murders
manni	person
margs	many
mat	food
með	along, as-well, with
meðan	while
mega	may
megi	may
mein	harm
meingerða	harmed
meinlætum	malignance
meir	more
menn	men, people
mér	I, me
messu	mass
mest	most
mestu	most
mik	me
mikil	much
mikill	large
mikils	much
mikinn	great
mikit	much
miklu	great, much
mín	my
mjök	a-great
mönnum	people
mösurtré	maple-tree
móti	return
mundi	should
mundið	remember
mundu	would
munnlaugar	mouth-basins
munum	shall
myrkri	darkness

N, n

Old Norse	English
nær	when
nærri	near
næstunni	the-last-time

Word List (Old Norse to English)

Old Norse	English
nætr	nights
nafnbót	rank
nafni	name, names
náttúru	the-nature
nema	without
nes	headland
niðr	down, son
njóta	enjoy
nokkurt	some
nokkut	anything
norðr	north
Noregi	Norway (place)
nótt	night
nú	now
nyt	use

O, o

Old Norse	English
ofan	above, down, over
ok	also, and
okkart	ours
olli	caused
orðit	become
orðum	words
Orminum	serpent
oss	us

Ó, ó

Old Norse	English
Óláf	Olaf (name)
Óláfr	Olaf (name)
Óláfs	Olaf (name)
ór	from, out-of, through
óvíst	uncertain

Ö, ö

Old Norse	English
öðru	the-other
öðrum	other
öl	ale
öll	all
öllu	all
öllum	all
önnur	also

P, p

Old Norse	English
prettóttr	deceitful

R, r

Old Norse	English
Rauðabergi	Raudaberg (place)
rauðum	red
reiðingr	riding
reiðir	angry
reiðklæðum	riding-clothes
reistu	raised
ríða	riders, riding, rode
risnu	hospitality

S, s

Old Norse	English
sá	saw
sæmiliga	well-enough
sængr	beds
sætis	seats
sagði	said, told
sagt	said
sama	the-same
saman	together
samnafna	same-name
samt	together
sat	sat
sé	is
seg	say
segir	said, told
segist	said
segja	said, say, to-say
sem	as, that-which
sendi	sends, sent
sendir	sent
sent	sent
sér	him, himself, saw, them
sét	seen
settu	set

Word List (Old Norse to English)

Old Norse	English
Síðan	after, afterwards, since, then
síðasta	last
síðr	less
siðu	customs
signa	signed
sik	themselves
silfri	silver
sína	his
sinn	his
sinni	with
síns	his, theirs
sínum	his, theirs
sitr	sat
Sjá	saw
sjaldan	seldom
sjó	the-sea
skal	shall
skamma	short
skammt	short-distance
skildum	separated
skilja	separate
skip	ship
skipinu	the-ship
skips	ships
skipsins	ship
skipta	divide
skjótliga	shortly
skjótt	away, quickly, shortly
skóginn	the-forest
skóginum	the-forest
skógr	forests
sköruligu	bold-like
skrautligri	splendid
skulu	shall
skulum	should
slík	such
slógu	threw
slökktu	put-out
smjör	butter
sonr	son
spurði	asked
spyrja	asked
spyrr	asked
stafat	staved
stafnana	ship's-prow

Old Norse	English
standa	stand, stood
stigu	stepped
stóð	stood
stöðva	stop
stofunni	the-room
Stöndum	stand
stöngin	the-pole
stóra	great
stund	time, while
Sú	so
suðr	south
sumri	summer
sumt	some
svá	so
svarar	answered
svíkja	fool
sýndi	showed
syni	sons

T, t

Old Norse	English
taka	take, took
tala	spoke
talit	counted
tekin	taken
tekr	took
tendruð	lit
tíðendi	news
tign	prestige
til	to, until
tjald	tent
tjaldi	tent
tók	received
tóku	took
tólf	twelve
trölla	monsters
tvá	two
tvau	two
tveir	two

Þ, þ

Old Norse	English
þá	them, then
þær	these, they

Word List (Old Norse to English)

Old Norse	English
þakkaði	thanked
þangat	from-there
þann	the
Þar	there
Þat	it, it-was, that, that, the
þau	them, they, those
þegar	as-soon-as, straight-away
þegn	thane
þeim	that, them, then, they
þeir	the, they
þeira	theirs, they
þenna	these, they
þér	to-you, you, you-to
Þess	this
þessa	this
Þessi	this
þessu	this
þetta	that, they, this
þigg	accept
þjóna	served
þó	though
Þóri	Thori (name)
Þórir	Thorir (name)
Þorsteinn	Thorstein (name)
þótt	thought
þótti	thinks, thought
þóttist	thought
þreyta	tired
þrifligir	thriving
þrír	three
þrjá	three
þrjár	three
þú	you
því	accordingly, because, because-of, therefore
þykkir	thought
þykkjast	realised
þykkju	things

U, u

um	about, in
undir	under
undr	strange
upp	up
Urðu	became

Ú, ú

úti	outside

V, v

væn	fair
vænleik	beauty
væri	should-be, was, were, would-be
værið	become
valdi	control
var	was, were
varða	warrant
varðveita	preserved
varir	aware
várr	aware, ours
váru	was, were
vatnskarl	basins
veðr	weather
veðrit	a-storm, weather
veg	way
Veit	knew
vel	well
vér	we
vera	be
verða	became, become, to-become, were
Verðr	became
verðum	have
verit	been
vetr	winter
vetrinn	winter
við	to, with
víða	widely
Víkinni	the-bay
vil	will, wish
vildi	wished, would
vildu	wished
vilduð	willed

Word List (Old Norse to English)

Old Norse	English
vill	wished
Vímund	Vimund (name)
vináttu	friendship
vinir	friend
vísa	directed
vissan	knowledge
vissi	knew
víst	certain
vísu	a-verse
vit	we, with
vita	certainly, know

Y, y

yðar	you
yðr	to-you, you, yours
yðra	yours
yðrar	yours
yfir	over
yfirstigna	surpassed
yrði	becomes

Ý, ý

ýmsum	various

Word List *(English to Old Norse)*

English	Old Norse

A, a

English	Old Norse
about	á, á
an	á
and	á, á, á, á, áðr, af
all	alla, allar, allgóðir, allgóðr, Allgott, allir, Allr, allra, allt
all-gold	allgóðir
all-good	allgóðr, Allgott
Alreksstead (place)	Alreksstöðum
another	annarr, annarrar, annat
after	aptni, at, at
at	at
a-farm	bæ
asked	beiddi, beiddi, beran, betr, betra
a-table	borð
a-crash	brest
away	brott, brottu, burt, byskup
a-day	dag
alone	einn
afterwards	eptir, er
am	er
are	er, er
as	er, er
are-you	ertu
above	framar, Frétti
at-sea	hafa
am-named	heiti
a-local-chief	hersir
attending	hlýða
any	hver
allowed	láta
a-man	maðr
along	með
as-well	með
a-great	mjök
anything	nokkut
also	ok, ok
ale	öl
angry	reiðir
answered	svarar
as-soon-as	þegar
accept	þigg
accordingly	því
aware	varir, várr
a-storm	veðrit
a-verse	vísu

B, b

English	Old Norse
by	á
before	áðr, af
bid	bað
both	báðir, bæ
bore	báru
bids	beiddi
bare	beran
better	betr, betra, betri
bright	bjart
bless	blessa
blind	blindr
brothers	bræðr
brother	bróðir, bróður
bishop	byskup
but	en
brought	færa
bring	færir
bacon	flesk
beautiful	fríðr
be	gerði, gerði
busy	heldu
beside	hjá
beds	hvílur, hyrfi
become	kominn, kominn, kominn, komit
bathed	laugat
bold-like	sköruligu
butter	smjör
because	því
because-of	því
became	Urðu, væn, vænleik

25

Word List (English to Old Norse)

English	Old Norse
beauty	vænleik
basins	vatnskarl
been	verit
becomes	yrði

C, c

crash	bresti
company	félögum
come	gakk, gat
could	gat
circumstances	hag
came	kæmi, kallaðir, kallat, kann, kastar, kemr, kenna
called	kallaðir, kallat
can	kann
cast	kastar
church	kirkju
church-door	kirkjudyra
chests	kistlar, kistlunum
clothed	klæðast
comes	komnir
colours	litum
concludes	lýkr
caused	olli
customs	siðu
counted	talit
control	valdi
certain	víst
certainly	vita

D, d

deeds	athöfn
day	dagr
dead	dauðum
darkness	dimma, dóttir
daughter	dóttir
daughter-of	dóttir, dóttur
dragon's-head	drekahöfuð
drank	drekka, drekka
drink	drekka, drekki, drepna, drykk

English	Old Norse
drinks	drykkinum
dwelled	dvaldist
directly	gegn
did	gera, gera, gera, gerði
do	gera
done	gera, gerði
daughter-of-Gudmund (name)	Guðmundardóttir
disappeared	hvarf, hvárrtveggi
down	niðr, njóta
deceitful	prettóttr
divide	skipta
directed	vísa

E, e

events	atburð
eighth	átti
eyes	augun
east	austan
extreme	býsna
enough	dugir
each	hvárrtveggi, hvárt
either	hvárt
evil	illa, illu
equal-length	jafnlengdar
evening	kveldit
enjoy	njóta

F, f

from	af, áliðnu, alla, allar, allgóðir
farm	bær
father	Faðir, fæðsla
feast	fæðsla
fair	fagrt, fám
few	fám
found	fann, fast
fastened	fast
fell	Fellr
Finnmark (place)	Finnmerkr
far-away	fjarri

Word List (English to Old Norse)

English	Old Norse
followers	fjölmenni
full	fullr
filled	fylla
for	fyrir
first	fyrra, fyrst
fashioned	gervar
from-where	hvaðan
food	krásir, kveðja
forests	skógr
fool	svíkja
from-there	þangat
friendship	vináttu
friend	vinir

G, g

English	Old Norse
got	fengi, Fengu
guard	gæta
gave	gaf
give	gefast
going	gengit, gengu
Glasir-Plains (place)	Glæsisvöllum
good	góð, góða, góðum, gott
graze	gras
gripped	greip
Gretti (name)	Gretti
Grim (name)	Gríma, Gríma
Grims' (name)	Gríma
Grims (name)	Grímar, Grímaskarð
Grim-Pass (place)	Grímaskarð
God	guð
Gudmund (name)	Guðmundar, Guðmundardóttir, Guðmundi
gold	gull, gullbúin
gold-inlaid	gullbúin
golden-ball	gullknappr
gold-laid	gullskotit
greatly	harðla
greeted	heilsar, heim
greetings	kveðju
great	mikinn, mikit, miklu

H, h

English	Old Norse
had	átti, augun, austan, bað, báðir, bæ, bæði, bær, baki
horseback	baki
has	hafi
held	Halda
her	hana, handlaugar
hand-washing	handlaugar
he	Hann, hann, hans
him	hann, hans, hans, hans
his	hans, harðla, heðan, hef, hefði
hence	heðan
have	hef, hefði, hefir, hefir
home	heim
Helga's (name)	Helga
Helgi (name)	Helga, Helgi
here	hér, herra
horses	hestanna, Hestar, hestum
heard	heyra, heyrðu, heyrt
heads	höfuðin
hands	höndum
horns	horn, hornin, hornum
how-so	Hversu
Hyrnings (name)	Hyrningar
harm	mein
harmed	meingerða
headland	nes
hospitality	risnu
himself	sér

I, i

English	Old Norse
in	á, á, áðr, af
it	á, áðr
if	ef
I	Ek, en
is	En, enda, Eptir
inquired	Frétti
Ingibjorg (name)	Ingibjörg, Ingibjörgu
it-was	þat

Word List (English to Old Norse)

English	Old Norse

K, k

English	Old Norse
killed	drápu, drekahöfuð
kinsman	frændum
keep	helzt
knew	kenna, kirkju, kirkjudyra
kinds-of	konar
kings	konunga
king	konungr
knowledge	vissan
know	vita

L, l

English	Old Norse
late	áliðnu
lord	herra
looked	horfði
locked	læsti
land	land, landi
land-tent	landtjaldinu
long	langa
longer	lengra
lived	lifir
laid	liggja
lay	liggja
lights	ljós, login
large	mikill
last	síðasta
less	síðr
lit	tendruð

M, m

English	Old Norse
more	fleiri, flesk
meet	fund
made	gerðu, gerir
may	má, maðr, maðr, mættið, mættum
man	maðr
murders	manndráp
many	margs
malignance	meinlætum
men	menn
me	mér, messu
mass	messu
most	mest, mestu
much	mikil, mikill, mikils, mikinn
my	mín
maple-tree	mösurtré
mouth-basins	munnlaugar
monsters	trölla

N, n

English	Old Norse
not	eigi, eigi, Ein
no	engi, engra
none	engum
noise	hark
named	heitir, heldr
nowhere	hvergi
near	nærri
nights	nætr
name	nafni
names	nafni
north	norðr
Norway (place)	Noregi
night	nótt
now	nú
news	tíðendi

O, o

English	Old Norse
of	á, á, á, á
on	á
out	á
others	aðrar
out-of	af, aflat
one	annarr, annarra, aptr, ár, at, at
other	annarra, aptr
or	eða
only	eigi
over	ofan, okkart
ours	okkart, Óláf

Word List (English to Old Norse)

English	Old Norse
Olaf (name)	Óláf, Óláfr, Óláfs
outside	úti

P, p

English	Old Norse
prayed	bað
prayers	bænir
prepared	búa, búin, búizt, búnar
passed	líðr
passes	líðr
properly	Makligr
people	manna, manna, manni
peoples	manna
person	manni
put-out	slökktu
prestige	tign
preserved	varðveita

Q, q

English	Old Norse
quickly	skjótt

R, r

English	Old Norse
returned	aptr
reason	gegndi
racket	hark
rather	heldr
room	herbergi
retainers	hirð
rest	hvílast
repay	launa
released	lausan
read	lesit
return	móti
remember	mundið
rank	nafnbót
Raudaberg (place)	Rauðabergi
red	rauðum
riding	reiðingr, reiðklæðum
riding-clothes	reiðklæðum

English	Old Norse
raised	reistu
riders	ríða
rode	ríða
realised	þykkjast
received	tók

S, s

English	Old Norse
so	á, á, aðrar
surplus	aflat
surpassed	bar, bjarga
settled	bjó
Sámi (name)	Finna
skilled-in-magic	fjölkunnigr
shone	glóaði
she	Hún
sports	íþróttir
spoke	kvað, kveðst, launa, lausan
said	kveðst, launa, lausan, leita, lesit, líðr
seeking	leita
should	mundi, mundið
shall	munum, nær, nærri
son	niðr, nokkurt
some	nokkurt, norðr
serpent	Orminum
saw	sá, sæmiliga, sætis
seats	sætis
same-name	samnafna
sat	sat, seg
say	seg, segir
sends	sendi
sent	sendi, sendir, sent
seen	sét
set	settu
since	síðan
signed	signa
silver	silfri
seldom	sjaldan
short	skamma
short-distance	skammt
separated	skildum
separate	skilja
ship	skip, skipinu

Word List (English to Old Norse)

English	Old Norse
ships	skips
shortly	skjótliga, skjótt
splendid	skrautligri
such	slík
staved	stafat
ship's-prow	stafnana
stand	standa, standa
stood	standa, stigu
stepped	stigu
stop	stöðva
south	suðr
summer	sumri
showed	sýndi
sons	syni
straight-away	þegar
served	þjóna
strange	undr
should-be	væri

T, t

English	Old Norse
to	á, aðrar, af, af, aflat
that	at, at, at, bað, bænir, bar, bjarga
the	at, at, bað, bænir, bar, bjarga, bjó, borð
to-save	bjarga
tables	borð
the-table	borða, borðum
the-brothers	bræðrum
the-bishop	byskup
the-dragon's-neck	drekahálsinum
the-drinks	drykkinum
than	en
then	En, en, engi, engra, engu
there-are	Eru
they-are	eru
travelled	færðu, færum, Fagna, fara, fara, farit, fé, ferr
travel	fara, fara
to-give	gefa
the-guests	Gestir
the-floor	gólfinu
the-Grims (name)	Grímar, Grímar
the-Grims' (name)	Grímar
treasures	gripir
the-hall	höllina
to-him	honum
the-horns	hornin, hornunum
thought	hugr, Hún, hvar, hvar, hvar
trade	kaupferð, kaupferð
trading-voyage	kaupferð
the-woman	kona
the-king	konung, konungi, Konungr, konungs
the-king's	konungs
to-lay	liggja
the-last-time	næstunni
the-nature	náttúru
the-other	öðru
through	ór
told	sagði, sagt
the-same	sama
together	saman, samnafna
to-say	segja
that-which	sem
them	sér, sét, settu, síðan
themselves	sik
theirs	síns, sínum, sitr
the-sea	sjó
the-ship	skipinu
the-forest	skóginn, skóginum
threw	slógu
the-room	stofunni
the-pole	stöngin
time	stund
take	taka
took	taka, tala, tekin
taken	tekin
these	þær, Þær
they	Þær, þakkaði, þann, Þar, þat, þat, þat
thanked	þakkaði
there	Þar
those	þau
thane	þegn
to-you	þér, þér
this	Þess, þessa, Þessi, þessu, þetta

Word List (English to Old Norse)

English	Old Norse	English	Old Norse
though	þó	went	ganga, gefa, gegndi
Thori (name)	Þóri	was-named	heita, heitir
Thorir (name)	Þórir	what	hvar, hvar
Thorstein (name)	Þorsteinn	why	Hví
thinks	þótti	woman	konu
tired	þreyta	women	konur, konurnar
thriving	þrifligir	with	með, meðan, menn, mönnum
three	þrír, þrjá, þrjár	while	meðan, menn
therefore	því	would	mundu, munum
things	þykkju	without	nema
tent	tjald, tjaldi	words	orðum
twelve	tólf	well-enough	sæmiliga
two	tvá, tvau, tveir	would-be	væri
to-become	verða	warrant	varða
the-bay	Víkinni	weather	veðr, veðrit
		way	veg
		well	vel
		we	vér, verða
		winter	vetr, vetrinn
		widely	víða
		will	vil
		wish	vil
		wished	vildi, vildi, vildu
		willed	vilduð

U, u

use	nyt
us	oss
uncertain	óvíst
until	til
under	undir
up	upp

V, v

vessels	ker
Vimund (name)	Vímund
various	ýmsum

W, w

was	en, engi, engra, engu, engum
were	er, er, er, er, er, Eru
when	er, er
where	er, er
which	er
who	er
we-are	Erum
welcomed	Fagna
wealth	fé, ferr

Y, y

year	ár
Yule	jól, jóla
you	þér, þér, Þess, þessa
you-to	þér
yours	yðr, yðra, yðrar

The Tale of Helgi Thórisson (Old Icelandic)

The Tale of Helgi Thórisson (*Old Icelandic*)

Old Icelandic	Literal	English
1	**1**	**1**
Þórir hét maður, er bjó í Noregi á bæ þeim, er á Rauðabergi heitir.	Thorir (name) was-named a-man, who settled in Norway (place) in a-farm that, was so Raudaberg (place) named.	There was a man named Thorir who lived in Norway on a farm that was named Raudaberg.
Þessi bær er skammt frá Víkinni.	This farm was short-distance from The-bay.	The farm was a short distance away from the bay.
Þórir átti tvá syni.	Thorir (name) had two sons.	Thorir had two sons.
Hét annar Helgi, en Þorsteinn annar; báðir voru þeir þrifligir menn, og var þó Helgi framar um íþróttir.	Was-named one Helgi (name), was Thorstein (name) another; both were they thriving men, and was though Helgi (name) above in sports.	One was named Helgi, the other was named Thorstein; they were both thriving men, though Helgi surpassed in sports.
Faðir þeirra var hersir að nafnbót.	Father theirs was a-local-chief of rank.	Their father was a local chief of high rank.
Hann var í vináttu við Óláf konung.	He was in friendship with Olaf (name) the-king.	He was friends with King Olaf.
Það var á einu sumri, að þeir bræður höfðu kaupferð norður til Finnmerkr og höfðu smjör og flesk til kaups við Finna.	it was in one summer, that the brothers had trading-voyage north to Finnmark (place) and had butter and bacon to trade with Sámi (name).	It was one summer, that the brothers had a trading voyage north to Finnmark, and they had butter and bacon to trade with the Sámi people.
Fengu þeir góða kaupferð og heldu aptr að áliðnu sumri og kómu um dag við nes það, er hét Vímund.	Got they good trade and busy returned in late summer and came about a-day to headland that, was named Vimund (name).	They had a good and busy trade and returned late in the summer and came about one day to a headland that was named Vimund.
Það var allgóður skógr.	there were all-good forests.	There were all-good woods.
Gengu þeir á land upp og fengu nokkurt mösurtré.	Went they to land up and got some maple-tree.	They went up to the land and got some maple trees.
Verður Helga lengra gengið í skóginn en öðrum mönnum.	Became Helgi (name) longer going in the-forest than other people.	Helgi went further into the woods than the other people.

The Tale of Helgi Thórisson (Old Icelandic)

Old Icelandic	Literal	English
Síðan kastar yfir myrkri miklu, svo að hann hittir ei til skipsins á þeim aptni; tekur nú og skjótt að dimma af nótt.	Then cast over darkness great, so that he found not to ship and then after; took now and quickly to darkness of night.	Then a great darkness cast over, so that he could not find the ship; and then afterwards the darkness of night took quickly.
Þá sért Helgi, hvar tólf konur ríða úr skóginum.	Then saw Helgi (name), were twelve women riding through the-forest.	Then Helgi saw that there were twelve women riding through the forest.
Þær voru allar á rauðum hestum og í rauðum reiðklæðum.	They were all on red horses and in red riding-clothes.	They were all on red horses and in red riding-clothes.
Þær stigu af baki.	They stepped from horseback.	They stepped down from their horses.
Allr reiðingr hestanna þá glóaði við gull.	All riding horses then shone with gold.	All the horses they were riding shone with gold.
Ein bar það af öllum um vænleik, og allar aðrar þjóna henni, þessi inni sköruligu konu.	One surpassed there of all about beauty, and all others served her, this the bold-like woman.	One of them surpassed all the others in beauty, and all the others served this bold looking woman.
Hestar þeirra gengu á gras.	Horses they went to graze.	The horses then went to graze.
Eptir það settu þær niður eitt fagrt tjald.	After that set they down one fair tent.	After that they set down a fair tent.
Var það stafat með ýmsum litum og víða gullskotit, og öll höfuðin voru við gull búin, er af upp gengu landtjaldinu, og svo stöngin, er upp stóð, og mikill gullknappr ofan á.	Was it staved with various colours and widely gold-laid, and all heads were with gold prepared, was of up going land-tent, and so the-pole, that up stood, and large golden-ball above it.	It was striped with various colours and widely laden with gold, and all the heads were prepared with gold, and so it was of this land tent, that all the poles that stood up had a large golden ball on top.
og er þær höfðu um búizt, reistu þær borð og báru á margs konar krásir.	and when they had about prepared, raised they a-table and bore out many kinds-of food.	And when they had prepared all about, they raised a table and brought our many kinds of food.
Þá tóku þær handlaugar, vatnskarl og munnlaugar, gervar af silfri, og allt laugat í gulli.	Then took they hand-washing, basins and mouth-basins, fashioned of silver, and all bathed in gold.	They took to washing their hands, with basins and jugs, fashioned of silver, and all bathed in gold.

The Tale of Helgi Thórisson (Old Icelandic)

Old Icelandic	Literal	English
Helgi stóð nærri tjaldi þeirra og horfði á.	Helgi (name) stood near tent theirs and looked about.	Helgi stood near their tent and looked about.
Sú, er fyrir þeim var, mælti:	So, was before them was, spoke:	The one who was in front of them spoke:
"Helgi, gakk hingað, og þigg hér mat og drykk með oss".	"Helgi (name), come here, and accept here food and drink with us".	"Helgi, come here, and accept food and drink with us".
Hann gerir svo.	He did so.	He did so.
Helgi sért, að það er fríður drykkr og önnur fæðsla og væn ker.	Helgi (name) saw, that there was beautiful drink and also feast and fair vessels.	Helgi saw that there were beautiful drinks and a feast with fair drinking vessels.
Þá voru borð ofan tekin og hvílur búnar, og voru þær miklu skrautligri en annarra manna sængr.	Then were tables down taken and beds prepared, and were these much splendid than other peoples beds.	Then the tables were taken down and the beds were prepared, and these were much more splendid than other peoples' beds.
Sú kona spyr Helga, er fyrir þeim var, hvort hann vildi heldur liggja einn saman eða hjá henni.	So the-woman asked Helgi (name), that for them was, either he wished rather to-lay alone together or beside her.	The woman who was at the front asked Helgi if he wished to lay alone or beside her.
Helgi spyr hana að nafni.	Helgi (name) asked her of name.	Helgi asked her name.
Hún svaraði:	She answered:	She answered:
"eg heiti Ingibjörg, dóttir Guðmundar af Glæsisvöllum".	"I am-named Ingibjorg (name), daughter Gudmund (name) of Glasir-Plains (place)".	"I am named Ingibjorg, daughter of Gudmund of Glasir Plains".
Helgi mælti:	Helgi (name) spoke:	Helgi spoke:
"Hjá þér vil eg liggja".	"Beside you wish I to-lay".	"I wish to lay beside you".
og svo gerðu þau þrjár nætr í samt.	and so did they three nights of together.	And so they did for three nights together.
Var þá bjart veður; standa þau þá upp og klæðast.	Was then bright weather; stood they then up and clothed.	When the weather was bright; they stood up and clothed.
Ingibjörg mælti þá:	Ingibjorg (name) spoke then:	Ingibjorg then spoke:

The Tale of Helgi Thórisson (Old Icelandic)

Old Icelandic	Literal	English
"Nú munum við hér skilja.	"Now shall we here separate.	"Now we shall separate here.
Eru hér kistlar tveir, annar er fullr af silfri, en annar af gulli, er eg vil gefi þér, og seg engum manni, hvaðan það kom".	There-are here chests two, one is full of silver, and another of gold, am I will to-give to-you, and say none person, from-where that came".	Here are two chests, one is full of silver, and another of gold, and I will give them to you, and you shall tell no person, where they came from".
Eptir það ríða þær burt sama veg sem þangað, en hann fór til skips síns.	After that rode they away the-same way as from-there, that he travelled to ships his.	After that they rode away the same way as they had come from, and he travelled to his ships.
Fagna þeir honum velkominn og spyrja, hvar hann dvaldist, en hann vilt það eigi frá segja.	Welcomed they him well and asked, where he dwelled, but he wished there not from to-say.	They welcomed him well and asked where he had stayed, but he did not wish to say.
Halda þeir þá suður með landi og koma heim til föður síns og hafi aflat mikils fjár.	Held they then south along land and came home to father theirs and had surplus much wealth.	They held south along the land and came to their father's home and had much wealth.
Faðir Helga og bróðir spyrja, hvaðan honum kom svo mikið fé sem hann hafði í kistlunum, en hann vilt það ei segja.	Father Helgi (name) and brother asked, from-where he came so much wealth as he had in chests, but he wished that not to-say.	Helgi's father and brother asked where he came by so much wealth as he had in his chests, but he did not wish to say.

2

Nú líður svo fram til jóla.	Now passed so from until Yule.	Now it passed on to Yule.
Það var eina nótt, að kemur á býsna veður.	it was one night, that came an extreme weather.	And it was one night that there came extreme weather.
Þorsteinn mælti við bróður sinn:	Thorstein (name) spoke with brother his:	Thorstein spoke with his brother:
"við skulum standa upp og viti, hvað líður um skip okkart".	"we should stand up and know, what passes about ship ours".	"We should get up and find out what is happening with our ship".
Þeir gera svo, og var það fast velkominn.	They did so, and was it fastened well.	They did so, and it was fastened well.

The Tale of Helgi Thórisson (Old Icelandic)

Old Icelandic	Literal	English
Helgi hafði látit gera drekahöfuð á skip þeirra upp á stafnana og búa velkominn fyrir ofan sjó.	Helgi (name) had made done dragon's-head on ship theirs up in ship's-prow and prepared well for above the-sea.	Helgi had a dragon's head made for their ship's prow and it was decorated well above the sea level.
Fór það fé það til, er Ingibjörg gaf honum, dóttir Guðmundar konungs, en sumt læsti hann í drekahálsinum.	Travelled the wealth there to, that Ingibjorg (name) gave him, daughter-of Gudmund (name) the-king, but some locked he in the-dragon's-neck.	The wealth that Ingibjorg, daughter of King Gudmund, gave him had travelled there but some of it was locked in the dragon's neck.
Þá heyra þeir brest mikinn.	Then heard they a-crash great.	Then they heard a great crash.
það ríða að þeim tveir menn og höfðu Helga í burt með sért.	there riders at them two men and had Helgi (name) to away with them.	Then two men rode towards them and took Helgi away with them.
Veit Þorsteinn ei, hvað af honum verður.	Knew Thorstein (name) not, what of him became.	Thorstein did not know what became of him.
Fellr þá veðrit skjótt.	Fell then weather away.	The weather then fell away.
Þorsteinn kemur heim og svarar föður sínum þenna atburð, og þykir þetta mikil tíðendi.	Thorstein (name) came home and told father his these events, and thought that much news.	Thorstein came home and told his father of these events, and thought that this news was very much.
fer hann þegar á fund Óláfs konungs og svarar honum, hvar komið var, og biður hann nú verða vissan um, hvar er sonur hans er niður kominn.	travelled he straight-away to meet Olaf (name) the-king and said to-him, what came was, and asked him now to-become knowledge about, where was son his and son become.	He travelled straight away to meet King Olaf and told him what had happened, and asked him for knowledge about where his son was and what had become of him.
konungur segist það gera mundu, sem hann beiddi, en kveðst þó óvíst hugr um segja, hver nyt frændum hans mundi að honum verða.	the-King said that do would, that-which he asked, but said though uncertain thought about said, any use kinsman he should to him become.	The king said that he would do what he asked, but said that it was uncertain to say, if his kinsman would be of any use after what had happened to him.
Síðan fór Þórir heim, og líður svo þetta ár og allt fram á jól annat ár, og situr konungur á Alreksstöðum um veturinn.	After travelled Thorir (name) home, and passed so that year and all from to Yule another year, and sat the-king in Alreksstead (place) about winter.	Afterwards Thorir travelled home, and so passed that year to Yule, and the king sat in Alreksstead over the winter.

The Tale of Helgi Thórisson (Old Icelandic)

Old Icelandic	Literal	English
Þá kemur átti dagr jóla, og um kveldið ganga þrír menn í höllina fyrir Óláf konung, þá er hann sat yfir borðum.	Then came eighth day Yule, and about evening went three men in the-hall before Olaf (name) the-king, then as he sat over the-table.	Then came the eighth day of Yule, and at about evening three men entered the hall before King Olaf, as he sat across the tables.
Þeir kveðja hann velkominn.	They greeted him well.	They greeted him well.
konungur heilsar þeim velkominn í móti.	the-King greeted them well in return.	The king greeted them well in return.
Er það kominn Helgi, en menn kenna ei hina tvá.	Then there came Helgi (name), but people knew not the two.	Then there came Helgi, but people did not know who the other two were.
konungur spurði þá að nafni, en hvárrtveggi kveðst Grímr heita.	the-King asked then the names, and each said Grim (name) was-named.	The king asked their names, and each said their name was Grim.
"Erum við sendir af Guðmundi á Glæsisvöllum hingað til yðar.	"We-are with sent of Gudmund (name) of Glasir-Plains (place) here to you.	"We have been sent by Gudmund of Glasir Plaines here to you.
Hann sendi yðurkveðju sína og það með tvö horn".	He sends you greetings his and there as-well two horns".	He sends you greetings and here as well two horns".
konungur tók við, og voru gullbúin.	the-King received with, and was gold-inlaid.	The king received them, and they were inlaid with gold.
Þetta voru allgóðir gripir.	They were all-gold treasures.	They were all good treasures.
Óláfr konungur átti tvö horn, er Hyrningar voru kallaðir, og þó að þau væri harðla góð, þá voru þau þó betri, er Guðmundr sendi honum.	Olaf (name) the-king had two horns, were Hyrnings (name) were called, and though that they were greatly good, then were they though better, that Gudmund (name) sent him.	King Olaf had two horns, that were called Hyrnings, and though they were great, the ones that Gudmund had sent him were better.
"Þess beiddi Guðmundr konungur yðvr, herra, að þér værið vinir hans, og þótti mestu varða um yðra þykkju, meir en allra annarra konunga".	"This bids Gudmund (name) the-king to-you, lord, that to-you become friend his, and thinks most warrant about yours things, more than all other kings".	"This Gudmund asks you, lord, that you become his friend, as he values you as more important than all other kings".
konungur svaraði þá öngu, en lætur vísa þeim til sætis félögum.	the-King answered then not, but had directed them to seats company.	The king did not answer then, but directed them to the seats with company.

The Tale of Helgi Thórisson (Old Icelandic)

Old Icelandic	Literal	English
konungur lætur fylla hornin Gríma af góðum drykk og lætur byskup blessa og lét færi þeim Grímum, að þeir drykki fyrst af.	the-King had filled the-horns Grim (name) of good drink and had bishop bless and had brought them Grims (name), that they drank first of.	The king had the Grim horns filled of good drink and had a bishop bless them and bring them to the Grims, so that they drank first.
Þá kvað konungur vísu þessa:	Then spoke the-king a-verse this:	Then the king spoke this verse:
"Gestir skulu hornum í gegn taka, meðan hvílast látum þenna þegn Guðmundar, og af samnafna sínum drekki; svo skal Grímum gott öl gefast".	"The-guests shall horns to directly take, while rest have they thane Gudmund (name), and of same-name theirs drink; so shall Grims (name) good ale give".	The guests shall these horns directly take, while they have rest thane of Gudmund, of his namesake theirs drink; so shall the Grims give good ale".
Þá taka Grímar við hornunum og þykjast nú viti, hvað byskup hefir yfir lesit drykkinum.	Then took Grims (name) with the-horns and realised now certainly, what the-bishop had over read drinks.	Then the Grims took the horns and realised now with certainty, what the bishop had read over these drinks.
Þeir segja þá:	They said then:	They then said:
"ei fer nú fjarri því, sem Guðmundr, konungur vor, gat til.	"not travel now far-away because, as Gudmund (name), the-king ours, could to.	"Now do not go far from what Gudmund, our king, could do.
Er þessi konungur prettóttr og kann illa gott að launa, því að konungur vor gerði til hans sæmiliga.	Is this king deceitful and can evil good to repay, therefore the king aware be to him well-enough.	This king is deceitful and repays good with evil, therefore the king should be well enough aware.
Stöndum nú upp allir og verðum í brottu héðan".	Stand now up all and have to away hence".	Let's get up and go right now".
svo gera þeir.	so did they.	They did so.
Verður þá hark mikið í stofunni.	Became then noise much in the-room.	Then there was much noise in the room.
Þeir slógu niður drykkinum af hornunum og slökktu login.	They threw down the-drinks of the-horns and put-out lights.	The threw down the drinks from the horns and put out the lights.
Þá heyrðu þeir bresti stóra.	Then heard they crash great.	Then they heard a great crash.

The Tale of Helgi Thórisson (Old Icelandic)

Old Icelandic	Literal	English
konungur bað guð til gæta og bað menn upp standa og stöðva þetta hark.	the-King prayed God to guard and bid men up stand and stop this racket.	The king prayed to God to guard him and asked his men to stand up and stop this racket.
Síðan verða þeir Grímar úti og Helgi með þeim.	Afterwards were they The-Grims (name) outside and Helgi (name) with them.	Afterwards the Grims were outside and Helgi was with them.
voru þá ljós upp tendruð í konungs herbergi.	were then lights up lit in the-king's room.	Then the lights were lit up in the king's room.
Sjá þeir þá drepna þrjá menn, en það liggja hornin Grímar á gólfinu hjá inum dauðum.	Saw they then killed three men, and there laid horns The-Grims' (name) by the-floor beside the dead.	They then saw that three men had been killed, and the Grims' horns were on the floor beside the dead.
"Þetta er undr mikið", sagði konungur, "og væri betur, að slík yrði sjaldan.	"This is strange much", said the-king, "and should-be better, that such becomes seldom.	"This is very strange", said the king, "and it would be best if this becomes seldom.
og það hef eg heyrt sagt af Guðmundi af Glæsisvöllum, að hann sé mjög fjölkunnigr og illu megi helst við hann skipta, og eru þeir menn illa komnir, er undir hans valdi eru, ef vér mættum nokkut að gera".	and that have I heard said of Gudmund (name) of Glasir-Plains (place), that he is a-great skilled-in-magic and evil may keep with him divide, and they-are the people evil comes, who under his control are, if we may anything to do".	And I have heard said of Gudmund of Glasir Plains, that he is greatly skilled in magic and his evil keeps dividing, and the people under his control are evil, even if anything may be done about it".
konungur lét varðveita hornin Gríma og af drekka, og dugir það velkominn.	the-king had preserved the-horns Grims' (name) and of drank, and enough it-was well.	The king had the Grim horns preserved and drank from them, and all was well enough.
það er nú kallat Grímaskarð ofan að Alreksstöðum, er þeir hafi austan farið, og er það engra manna að fara það síðan.	there is now called Grim-Pass (place) over at Alreksstead (place), where they had east travelled, and is that no people to travel there since.	There is a mountain pass called Grim Pass over at Alreksstead where they travelled east, and no people have travelled there since.

3

Nú líður af veturinn, og kemur annar átti dagr jóla, og er konungur í kirkju og hirð hans að hlýða messu.	Now passed of winter, and came another eighth day Yule, and was the-king in church and retainers his at attending mass.	Now it passed to winter, and another eighth day of Yule, and the king was in church with his retainers attending mass.

The Tale of Helgi Thórisson (Old Icelandic)

Old Icelandic	Literal	English
Þá koma það þrír menn til kirkjudyra, og er einn eptir, en tveir fara í brott og mæla þetta áður:	Then came there three men to church-door, and was one after, but two travelled to away and spoke this before:	Then there came three men to the church door, one of they stayed behind, but two travelled away and said before they went:
"Hér færum við þér Gretti, konungur, og er ei víst, nær þú færir af þér".	"Here travelled with to-you Gretti (name), king, and that not certain, when you bring out-of you-to".	"Here we bring to you Gretti, king, and it is not certain how you will be able to get rid of him".
Kenna menn það Helga.	Knew people there Helgi (name).	People came to know that it was Helgi.
Síðan gengur konungur til borða, og er menn tala við Helga, verða menn þess varir, að hann er blindr.	Afterwards went the-king to the-table, and as people spoke with Helgi (name), became people this aware, that he was blind.	Afterwards the king went to the tables, and as people spoke with Helgi, the became aware, that he was blind.
Frétti konungur þá, hverju gegndi um hans hag eða hvar hann hefðu verið þessa stund alla.	Inquired the-king then, each reason about his circumstances and where he had been this time all.	The king then inquired about each of the reasons of his circumstances and where he had been all this time.
Hann svarar þá konungi fyrst frá því, er hann fann konurnar í skóginum, þá frá því, er þeir Grímar gerðu veðrit að þeim bræðrum, er þeir vildu bjarga skipinu, og síðan höfðu þeir Grímar hann með sért til Guðmundar á Glæsisvöllum og færðu hann Ingibjörgu, dóttur Guðmundar.	He told then the-king first from accordingly, and he found women in the-forest, then from accordingly, that they The-Grims (name) made a-storm that they the-brothers, and they wished to-save the-ship, and afterwards had they The-Grims (name) him along himself to Gudmund (name) of Glasir-Plains (place) and travelled he Ingibjorg (name), daughter-of Gudmund (name).	He told the king accordingly from the beginning, how he found the women in the forest, that the Grims who were brothers had made a storm come upon the brothers, and how they wishes to save their ship, and afterwards how they took him to Gudmund of Glasir Plains and delivered him to Ingibjorg, daughter of Gudmund.
Þá mælti konungur:	Then spoke the-king:	Then the king spoke:
"Hversu þótti þér það að vera?"	"How-so thought you there to be?"	"How did you find it there?",
"Allgott", svarar hann, "og hvergi hefir mér betra þótt".	"All-good", said he, "and nowhere have I better thought".	"All good", said he, "and nowhere have I thought better".
Þá spurði konungur að um siðu Guðmundar konungs og að fjölmenni eða athöfn.	Then asked the-king that about customs Gudmund (name) the-king and to followers or deeds.	Then the king asked about the customs of Gudmund and his followers and their deeds.

The Tale of Helgi Thórisson (Old Icelandic)

Old Icelandic	Literal	English
En hann lét yfir öllu velkominn og sagði, að hans var miklu fleiri en hann fengi talit.	Then he had over all well and said, that he was much more than he got counted.	Then he had said well about all, and that there was more than he could count to tell them.
konungur mælti:	the-king spoke:	The king spoke:
"Hví fóru þér svo skjótliga í brott í fyrra vetur?"	"Why travelled you so shortly to away the first winter?"	"Why did you travel away so quickly the first winter?",
"Guðmundr konungur sendi þá til að svíkja yðor", svarar hann, "en fyrir bænir yðrar lét hann mig lausan, svo að þér mættið viti, hvað er af mér væri orðið.	"Gudmund (name) the-king sent them to of fool you", said he, "but for prayers yours had he me released, so that you may know, what was of me was become.	"King Gudmund sent them to fool you", he said, "but for your prayers he had me released, so that you may know what had become of me.
En því fóru vér svo skjótt í brott næstunni, að þeir Grímar höfðu ei náttúru til að drekka þann drykk, er þér létuð signa.	But because travelled we so shortly to away the-last-time, that they The-Grims (name) had not the-nature to of drink the drink, which you had signed.	But because we travelled so quickly away the last time, the Grims did not have the nature to drink the drink that you had signed.
Urðu þeir þessu reiðir, að þeir sá sig yfirstigna, og því drápu þeir menn yðra, að svo sagði Guðmundr konungur fyrir, ef þeir fengi eigi mein yður gert.	Became they this angry, that they saw themselves surpassed, and therefore killed they people yours, that so told Gudmund (name) the-king before, if they got not harm yours done.	They became angry that you had surpassed them, and therefore they killed your people, because King Gudmund told them to do so, if they could not do harm to you.
En hann sýndi tign sína í því, að hann sendi yður hornin, að þér mundið þá síður eptir mér leita".	But he showed prestige his in because, that he sent you the-horns, that you remember then less afterwards me seeking".	But he showed his prestige in sending you the horns, so that you would remember less about seeking me".
konungur spurði:	the-king asked:	The king asked:
"Hví fórtu nú í brott öðru sinni?"	"Why travelled now to away the-other with?"	"Why did you go away this time?",
Hann svaraði:	He answered:	he answered:
"Ingibjörg olli því.	"Ingibjorg (name) caused therefore.	"Because of Ingibjorg.

41

The Tale of Helgi Thórisson (Old Icelandic)

Old Icelandic	Literal	English
Hún þóttist ei mega liggja hjá mér nema með meinlætum, ef hún kæmi við mig beran, og því fór eg mest í brott, enda vildi Guðmundr konungur eigi þreyta við yður, þegar hann vissi, að þér vilduð mig í brott hafi.	She thought not may lay beside me without with malignance, if she came with me bare, and because-of travelled I most to away, and wished Gudmund (name) the-king not tired with you, as-soon-as he knew, that you willed me to away at-sea.	She thought that she may no longer lay beside me without feeling uneasy whenever she came into contact with me bare, and for that reason most I travelled away, and King Gudmund did not wise to be tired of you, as soon as he knew that you willed me to go away to sea.
En um tign og risnu Guðmundar konungs má eg ei í fám orðum segja og um fjölmenni það, er með honum er".	But about prestige and hospitality Gudmund (name) the-king may I only of few words to-say and about followers that, are with him are".	But about the prestige and hospitality of King Gudmund I have little words to say about it or the followers that are with him there".
konungur spurði:	the-king asked:	The king asked:
"Hví ertu blindr?"	"Why are-you blind?"	"Why are you blind?"
Hann svaraði:	He answered:	He answered:
"Ingibjörg Guðmundardóttir greip úr mér bæði augun, þá er við skildum, og sagði, að konur í Noregi mundu mín skamma stund njóta".	"Ingibjorg (name) Daughter-of-Gudmund (name) gripped from me both eyes, then when we separated, and said, that women in Norway (place) would my short while enjoy".	"Ingibjorg, daughter of Gudmund, gripped both my eyes from me, and then when we separated, she said that women in Norway would enjoy my company for a short while".
konungur sagði:	the-king said:	The king said:
"Makligr væri Guðmundr meingerða af mér fyrir þau manndráp, er hann gerði, ef guð vildi það vera láta".	"Properly would-be Gudmund (name) harmed of me for those murders, that he did, if God would that be allowed".	"Gudmund would be properly harmed by me for those murders that he did, if God would allow it".
Síðan var sent eptir Þóri, föður Helga, og þakkaði hann honum velkominn, er sonur hans var aptr kominn úr trölla höndum.	Afterwards was sent after Thori (name), father Helga's (name), and thanked he him well, that son his was returned come from monsters hands.	Afterwards Helgi's father Thorri was sent for and he thanked him well that his son was returned from the hands of such monsters.
fer hann síðan heim, en Helgi er eptir með konungi og lifir til annarrar jafnlengdar.	travelled he then home, but Helgi (name) was after with the-king and lived until another equal-length.	He then travelled home, but Helgi was thereafter with the king and lived another year.

The Tale of Helgi Thórisson (Old Icelandic)

Old Icelandic	Literal	English
En konungur hefir hornin Gríma með sért, þá er hann fór síðasta sinn úr landi.	Then the-king had the-horns Grims' (name) with him, then when he travelled last his out-of land.	Then the king had the Grim horns with him, when he travelled last out of the land.
En það segja menn, þá er Óláfr konungur hvarf af Orminum langa, að hyrfi og hornin og hafi engi maður þau séð síðan.	Is it said people, then that Olaf (name) the-king disappeared from Serpent long, that disappeared also the-horns and has no man them seen since.	It is said by people, that then King Olaf disappeared from The Long Serpent, and that the horns also disappeared and no man has seen them since.
og lýkr hér frá Grímum að segja.	and concludes here from The-Grims (name) to say.	And here concludes what may be said about the Grims.

Word List *(Old Icelandic to English)*

Old Icelandic	English
A, a	
að	at, in, of, that, the, to
aðrar	others
af	from, of, out-of
aflat	surplus
alla	all
allar	all
allgóðir	all-gold
allgóður	all-good
Allgott	all-good
allir	all
Allr	all
allra	all
allt	all
Alreksstöðum	Alreksstead (place)
annar	another, one
annarra	other
annarrar	another
annat	another
aptni	after
aptr	returned
atburð	events
athöfn	deeds
augun	eyes
austan	east
Á, á	
á	about, an, and, by, in, it, of, on, out, so, to
áður	before
áliðnu	late
ár	year
átti	eighth, had
B, b	
bað	bid, prayed
báðir	both

Old Icelandic	English
bæ	a-farm
bæði	both
bænir	prayers
bær	farm
baki	horseback
bar	surpassed
báru	bore
beiddi	asked, bids
beran	bare
betra	better
betri	better
betur	better
biður	asked
bjarga	to-save
bjart	bright
bjó	settled
blessa	bless
blindr	blind
borð	a-table, tables
borða	the-table
borðum	the-table
bræðrum	the-brothers
bræður	brothers
brest	a-crash
bresti	crash
bróðir	brother
bróður	brother
brott	away
brottu	away
búa	prepared
búin	prepared
búizt	prepared
búnar	prepared
burt	away
byskup	bishop, the-bishop
býsna	extreme
D, d	
dag	a-day
dagr	day
dauðum	dead

44

Word List (Old Icelandic to English)

Old Icelandic	English
dimma	darkness
dóttir	daughter, daughter-of
dóttur	daughter-of
drápu	killed
drekahálsinum	the-dragon's-neck
drekahöfuð	dragon's-head
drekka	drank, drink
drekki	drink
drepna	killed
drykk	drink
drykki	drank
drykkinum	drinks, the-drinks
drykkr	drink
dugir	enough
dvaldist	dwelled

E, e

Old Icelandic	English
eða	and, or
ef	if
eg	I
ei	not, only
eigi	not
Ein	one
eina	one
einn	alone, one
einu	one
eitt	one
en	and, but, is, than, that, then, was
enda	and
engi	no
engra	no
engum	none
Eptir	after, afterwards
er	am, and, are, as, is, that, then, was, were, when, where, which, who
ertu	are-you
eru	are, there-are, they-are
Erum	we-are

F, f

Old Icelandic	English
Faðir	father
fæðsla	feast
færðu	travelled
færi	brought
færir	bring
færum	travelled
Fagna	welcomed
fagrt	fair
fám	few
fann	found
fara	travel, travelled
farið	travelled
fast	fastened
fé	wealth
Fellr	fell
félögum	company
fengi	got
Fengu	got
fer	travel, travelled
Finna	Sámi (name)
Finnmerkr	Finnmark (place)
fjár	wealth
fjarri	far-away
fjölkunnigr	skilled-in-magic
fjölmenni	followers
fleiri	more
flesk	bacon
föður	father
fór	travelled
fórtu	travelled
fóru	travelled
frá	from
frændum	kinsman
fram	from, from
framar	above
Frétti	inquired
fríður	beautiful
fullr	full
fund	meet
fylla	filled
fyrir	before, for
fyrra	first
fyrst	first

Word List (Old Icelandic to English)

Old Icelandic	English

G, g

gæta	guard
gaf	gave
gakk	come
ganga	went
gat	could
gefast	give
gefi	to-give
gegn	directly
gegndi	reason
gengið	going
gengu	going, went
gengur	went
gera	did, do, done
gerði	be, did
gerðu	did, made
gerir	did
gert	done
gervar	fashioned
Gestir	the-guests
Glæsisvöllum	Glasir-Plains (place)
glóaði	shone
góð	good
góða	good
góðum	good
gólfinu	the-floor
gott	good
gras	graze
greip	gripped
Gretti	Gretti (name)
Gríma	Grim (name), Grims' (name)
Grímar	Grims (name), the-Grims (name), the-Grims' (name)
Grímaskarð	Grim-Pass (place)
Grímr	Grim (name)
Grímum	Grims (name), the-Grims (name)
gripir	treasures
guð	God
Guðmundar	Gudmund (name)
Guðmundardóttir	daughter-of-Gudmund (name)
Guðmundi	Gudmund (name)
Guðmundr	Gudmund (name)
gull	gold
gullbúin	gold-inlaid
gulli	gold
gullknappr	golden-ball
gullskotit	gold-laid

H, h

hafði	had
hafi	at-sea, had, has
hag	circumstances
Halda	held
hana	her
handlaugar	hand-washing
Hann	he, him
hans	he, him, his
harðla	greatly
hark	noise, racket
héðan	hence
hef	have
hefðu	had
hefir	had, have
heilsar	greeted
heim	home
heita	was-named
heiti	am-named
heitir	named
heldu	busy
heldur	rather
Helga	Helga's (name), Helgi (name)
Helgi	Helgi (name)
helst	keep
henni	her
hér	here
herbergi	room
herra	lord
hersir	a-local-chief
hestanna	horses
Hestar	horses
hestum	horses

Word List (Old Icelandic to English)

Old Icelandic	English
hét	named, was-named
heyra	heard
heyrðu	heard
heyrt	heard
hina	the
hingað	here
hirð	retainers
hittir	found
hjá	beside
hlýða	attending
höfðu	had
höfuðin	heads
höllina	the-hall
höndum	hands
honum	he, him, to-him
horfði	looked
horn	horns
hornin	horns, the-horns
hornum	horns
hornunum	the-horns
hugr	thought
Hún	she
hvað	what
hvaðan	from-where
hvar	were, what, where
hvarf	disappeared
hvárrtveggi	each
hver	any
hvergi	nowhere
hverju	each
Hversu	how-so
Hví	why
hvílast	rest
hvílur	beds
hvort	either
hyrfi	disappeared
Hyrningar	Hyrnings (name)

I, i

Old Icelandic	English
illa	evil
illu	evil
Ingibjörg	Ingibjorg (name)
Ingibjörgu	Ingibjorg (name)
inni	the
inum	the

Í, í

Old Icelandic	English
í	in, of, the, to
íþróttir	sports

J, j

Old Icelandic	English
jafnlengdar	equal-length
jól	Yule
jóla	Yule

K, k

Old Icelandic	English
kæmi	came
kallaðir	called
kallat	called
kann	can
kastar	cast
kaupferð	trade, trading-voyage
kaups	trade
kemur	came
kenna	knew
ker	vessels
kirkju	church
kirkjudyra	church-door
kistlar	chests
kistlunum	chests
klæðast	clothed
kom	came
koma	came
komið	came
kominn	become, came, come
komnir	comes
kómu	came
kona	the-woman
konar	kinds-of
konu	woman
konung	the-king
konunga	kings
konungi	the-king
konungs	the-king, the-king's

Word List (Old Icelandic to English)

Old Icelandic	English
konungur	king, the-King
konur	women
konurnar	women
krásir	food
kvað	spoke
kveðja	greeted
kveðju	greetings
kveðst	said
kveldið	evening

L, l

Old Icelandic	English
læsti	locked
lætur	had
land	land
landi	land
landtjaldinu	land-tent
langa	long
láta	allowed
látit	made
látum	have
laugat	bathed
launa	repay
lausan	released
leita	seeking
lengra	longer
lesit	read
lét	had
létuð	had
líður	passed, passes
lifir	lived
liggja	laid, lay, to-lay
litum	colours
ljós	lights
login	lights
lýkr	concludes

M, m

Old Icelandic	English
má	may
maður	a-man, man
mæla	spoke
mælti	spoke
mættið	may
mættum	may
Makligr	properly
manna	people, peoples
manndráp	murders
manni	person
margs	many
mat	food
með	along, as-well, with
meðan	while
mega	may
megi	may
mein	harm
meingerða	harmed
meinlætum	malignance
meir	more
menn	men, people
mér	I, me
messu	mass
mest	most
mestu	most
mig	me
mikið	much
mikil	much
mikill	large
mikils	much
mikinn	great
miklu	great, much
mín	my
mjög	a-great
mönnum	people
mösurtré	maple-tree
móti	return
mundi	should
mundið	remember
mundu	would
munnlaugar	mouth-basins
munum	shall
myrkri	darkness

N, n

Old Icelandic	English
nær	when
nærri	near
næstunni	the-last-time
nætr	nights

Word List (Old Icelandic to English)

Old Icelandic	English
nafnbót	rank
nafni	name, names
náttúru	the-nature
nema	without
nes	headland
niður	down, son
njóta	enjoy
nokkurt	some
nokkut	anything
norður	north
Noregi	Norway (place)
nótt	night
nú	now
nyt	use

O, o

Old Icelandic	English
ofan	above, down, over
og	also, and
okkart	ours
olli	caused
orðið	become
orðum	words
Orminum	serpent
oss	us

Ó, ó

Old Icelandic	English
Óláf	Olaf (name)
Óláfr	Olaf (name)
Óláfs	Olaf (name)
óvíst	uncertain

Ö, ö

Old Icelandic	English
öðru	the-other
öðrum	other
öl	ale
öll	all
öllu	all
öllum	all
öngu	not
önnur	also

P, p

Old Icelandic	English
prettóttr	deceitful

R, r

Old Icelandic	English
Rauðabergi	Raudaberg (place)
rauðum	red
reiðingr	riding
reiðir	angry
reiðklæðum	riding-clothes
reistu	raised
ríða	riders, riding, rode
risnu	hospitality

S, s

Old Icelandic	English
sá	saw
sæmiliga	well-enough
sængr	beds
sætis	seats
sagði	said, told
sagt	said
sama	the-same
saman	together
samnafna	same-name
samt	together
sat	sat
sé	is
séð	seen
seg	say
segist	said
segja	said, say, to-say
sem	as, that-which
sendi	sends, sent
sendir	sent
sent	sent
sért	him, himself, saw, them
settu	set
Síðan	after, afterwards, since, then

Word List (Old Icelandic to English)

Old Icelandic	English	Old Icelandic	English
síðasta	last	stigu	stepped
siðu	customs	stóð	stood
síður	less	stöðva	stop
sig	themselves	stofunni	the-room
signa	signed	Stöndum	stand
silfri	silver	stöngin	the-pole
sína	his	stóra	great
sinn	his	stund	time, while
sinni	with	Sú	so
síns	his, theirs	suður	south
sínum	his, theirs	sumri	summer
situr	sat	sumt	some
Sjá	saw	svaraði	answered
sjaldan	seldom	svarar	said, told
sjó	the-sea	svíkja	fool
skal	shall	svo	so
skamma	short	sýndi	showed
skammt	short-distance	syni	sons
skildum	separated		
skilja	separate		
skip	ship	**T, t**	
skipinu	the-ship		
skips	ships	taka	take, took
skipsins	ship	tala	spoke
skipta	divide	talit	counted
skjótliga	shortly	tekin	taken
skjótt	away, quickly, shortly	tekur	took
skóginn	the-forest	tendruð	lit
skóginum	the-forest	tíðendi	news
skógr	forests	tign	prestige
sköruligu	bold-like	til	to, until
skrautligri	splendid	tjald	tent
skulu	shall	tjaldi	tent
skulum	should	tók	received
slík	such	tóku	took
slógu	threw	tólf	twelve
slökktu	put-out	trölla	monsters
smjör	butter	tvá	two
sonur	son	tveir	two
spurði	asked	tvö	two
spyr	asked		
spyrja	asked	**Þ, þ**	
stafat	staved		
stafnana	ship's-prow	þá	them, then
standa	stand, stood		

Word List (Old Icelandic to English)

Old Icelandic	English
það	it, it-was, that, the, there
þær	these, they
þakkaði	thanked
þangað	from-there
þann	the
þau	them, they, those
þegar	as-soon-as, straight-away
þegn	thane
þeim	that, them, then, they
þeir	the, they
þeirra	theirs, they
þenna	these, they
þér	to-you, you, you-to
Þess	this
þessa	this
Þessi	this
þessu	this
þetta	that, they, this
þigg	accept
þjóna	served
þó	though
Þóri	Thori (name)
Þórir	Thorir (name)
Þorsteinn	Thorstein (name)
þótt	thought
þótti	thinks, thought
þóttist	thought
þreyta	tired
þrifligir	thriving
þrír	three
þrjá	three
þrjár	three
þú	you
því	accordingly, because, because-of, therefore
þykir	thought
þykjast	realised
þykkju	things

U, u

Old Icelandic	English
um	about, in
undir	under
undr	strange
upp	up
Urðu	became

Ú, ú

Old Icelandic	English
úr	from, out-of, through
úti	outside

V, v

Old Icelandic	English
væn	fair
vænleik	beauty
væri	should-be, was, were, would-be
værið	become
valdi	control
var	was, were
varða	warrant
varðveita	preserved
varir	aware
vatnskarl	basins
veðrit	a-storm, weather
veður	weather
veg	way
Veit	knew
velkominn	well
vér	we
vera	be
verða	became, become, to-become, were
verðum	have
Verður	became
verið	been
vetur	winter
veturinn	winter
við	to, we, with
víða	widely
Víkinni	the-bay
vil	will, wish
vildi	wished, would
vildu	wished
vilduð	willed
vilt	wished

Word List (Old Icelandic to English)

Old Icelandic	English
Vímund	Vimund (name)
vináttu	friendship
vinir	friend
vísa	directed
vissan	knowledge
vissi	knew
víst	certain
vísu	a-verse
viti	certainly, know
vor	aware, ours
voru	was, were

Y, y

yðar	you
yðra	yours
yðrar	yours
yður	to-you, you, yours
yfir	over
yfirstigna	surpassed
yrði	becomes

Ý, ý

ýmsum	various

Word List *(English to Old Icelandic)*

English	Old Icelandic
A, a	
about	á, um
above	framar, ofan
accept	þigg
accordingly	því
a-crash	brest
a-day	dag
a-farm	bæ
after	aptni, Eptir, Síðan
afterwards	eptir, Síðan
a-great	mjög
ale	öl
all	alla, allar, allir, Allr, allra, allt, öll, öllu, öllum
all-gold	allgóðir
all-good	allgóður, Allgott
allowed	láta
a-local-chief	hersir
alone	einn
along	með
Alreksstead (place)	Alreksstöðum
also	og, önnur
am	er
a-man	maður
am-named	heiti
an	á
and	á, eða, en, enda, er, og
angry	reiðir
another	annar, annarrar, annat
answered	svaraði
any	hver
anything	nokkut
are	er, eru
are-you	ertu
as	er, sem
asked	beiddi, biður, spurði, spyr, spyrja
as-soon-as	þegar
a-storm	veðrit
as-well	með
at	að
a-table	borð
at-sea	hafi
attending	hlýða
a-verse	vísu
aware	varir, vor
away	brott, brottu, burt, skjótt
B, b	
bacon	flesk
bare	beran
basins	vatnskarl
bathed	laugat
be	gerði, vera
beautiful	fríður
beauty	vænleik
became	Urðu, verða, Verður
because	því
because-of	því
become	kominn, orðið, værið, verða
becomes	yrði
beds	hvílur, sængr
been	verið
before	áður, fyrir
beside	hjá
better	betra, betri, betur
bid	bað
bids	beiddi
bishop	byskup
bless	blessa
blind	blindr
bold-like	sköruligu
bore	báru
both	báðir, bæði
bright	bjart
bring	færir
brother	bróðir, bróður
brothers	bræður

Word List (English to Old Icelandic)

English	Old Icelandic
brought	færi
busy	heldu
but	en
butter	smjör
by	á

C, c

called	kallaðir, kallat
came	kæmi, kemur, kom, koma, komið, kominn, kómu
can	kann
cast	kastar
caused	olli
certain	víst
certainly	viti
chests	kistlar, kistlunum
church	kirkju
church-door	kirkjudyra
circumstances	hag
clothed	klæðast
colours	litum
come	gakk, kominn
comes	komnir
company	félögum
concludes	lýkr
control	valdi
could	gat
counted	talit
crash	bresti
customs	siðu

D, d

darkness	dimma, myrkri
daughter	dóttir
daughter-of	dóttir, dóttur
daughter-of-Gudmund (name)	Guðmundardóttir
day	dagr
dead	dauðum
deceitful	prettóttr
deeds	athöfn

English	Old Icelandic
did	gera, gerði, gerðu, gerir
directed	vísa
directly	gegn
disappeared	hvarf, hyrfi
divide	skipta
do	gera
done	gera, gert
down	niður, ofan
dragon's-head	drekahöfuð
drank	drekka, drykki
drink	drekka, drekki, drykk, drykkr
drinks	drykkinum
dwelled	dvaldist

E, e

each	hvárrtveggi, hverju
east	austan
eighth	átti
either	hvort
enjoy	njóta
enough	dugir
equal-length	jafnlengdar
evening	kveldið
events	atburð
evil	illa, illu
extreme	býsna
eyes	augun

F, f

fair	fagrt, væn
far-away	fjarri
farm	bær
fashioned	gervar
fastened	fast
father	Faðir, föður
feast	fæðsla
fell	Fellr
few	fám
filled	fylla
Finnmark (place)	Finnmerkr

Word List (English to Old Icelandic)

English	Old Icelandic
first	fyrra, fyrst
followers	fjölmenni
food	krásir, mat
fool	svíkja
for	fyrir
forests	skógr
found	fann, hittir
friend	vinir
friendship	vináttu
from	af, frá, fram, fram, úr
from-there	þangað
from-where	hvaðan
full	fullr

G, g

English	Old Icelandic
gave	gaf
give	gefast
Glasir-Plains (place)	Glæsisvöllum
God	guð
going	gengið, gengu
gold	gull, gulli
golden-ball	gullknappr
gold-inlaid	gullbúin
gold-laid	gullskotit
good	góð, góða, góðum, gott
got	fengi, Fengu
graze	gras
great	mikinn, miklu, stóra
greatly	harðla
greeted	heilsar, kveðja
greetings	kveðju
Gretti (name)	Gretti
Grim (name)	Gríma, Grímr
Grim-Pass (place)	Grímaskarð
Grims (name)	Grímar, Grímum
Grims' (name)	Gríma
gripped	greip
guard	gæta
Gudmund (name)	Guðmundar, Guðmundi, Guðmundr

H, h

English	Old Icelandic
had	átti, hafði, hafi, hefðu, hefir, höfðu, lætur, lét, létuð
hands	höndum
hand-washing	handlaugar
harm	mein
harmed	meingerða
has	hafi
have	hef, hefir, látum, verðum
he	Hann, hans, honum
headland	nes
heads	höfuðin
heard	heyra, heyrðu, heyrt
held	Halda
Helga's (name)	Helga
Helgi (name)	Helga, Helgi
hence	héðan
her	hana, henni
here	hér, hingað
him	hann, hans, honum, sért
himself	sért
his	hans, sína, sinn, síns, sínum
home	heim
horns	horn, hornin, hornum
horseback	baki
horses	hestanna, Hestar, hestum
hospitality	risnu
how-so	Hversu
Hyrnings (name)	Hyrningar

I, i

English	Old Icelandic
I	eg, mér
if	ef
in	á, að, í, um
Ingibjorg (name)	Ingibjörg, Ingibjörgu
inquired	Frétti
is	En, er, sé
it	á, það

Word List (English to Old Icelandic)

English	Old Icelandic
it-was	það

K, k

English	Old Icelandic
keep	helst
killed	drápu, drepna
kinds-of	konar
king	konungur
kings	konunga
kinsman	frændum
knew	kenna, Veit, vissi
know	viti
knowledge	vissan

L, l

English	Old Icelandic
laid	liggja
land	land, landi
land-tent	landtjaldinu
large	mikill
last	síðasta
late	áliðnu
lay	liggja
less	síður
lights	ljós, login
lit	tendruð
lived	lifir
locked	læsti
long	langa
longer	lengra
looked	horfði
lord	herra

M, m

English	Old Icelandic
made	gerðu, látit
malignance	meinlætum
man	maður
many	margs
maple-tree	mösurtré
mass	messu
may	má, mættið, mættum, mega, megi
me	mér, mig
meet	fund
men	menn
monsters	trölla
more	fleiri, meir
most	mest, mestu
mouth-basins	munnlaugar
much	mikið, mikil, mikils, miklu
murders	manndráp
my	mín

N, n

English	Old Icelandic
name	nafni
named	heitir, hét
names	nafni
near	nærri
news	tíðendi
night	nótt
nights	nætr
no	engi, engra
noise	hark
none	engum
north	norður
Norway (place)	Noregi
not	ei, eigi, öngu
now	nú
nowhere	hvergi

O, o

English	Old Icelandic
of	á, að, af, í
Olaf (name)	Óláf, Óláfr, Óláfs
on	á
one	annar, Ein, eina, einn, einu, eitt
only	ei
or	eða
other	annarra, öðrum
others	aðrar
ours	okkart, vor
out	á
out-of	af, úr

Word List (English to Old Icelandic)

English	Old Icelandic
outside	úti
over	ofan, yfir

P, p

English	Old Icelandic
passed	líður
passes	líður
people	manna, menn, mönnum
peoples	manna
person	manni
prayed	bað
prayers	bænir
prepared	búa, búin, búizt, búnar
preserved	varðveita
prestige	tign
properly	Makligr
put-out	slökktu

Q, q

English	Old Icelandic
quickly	skjótt

R, r

English	Old Icelandic
racket	hark
raised	reistu
rank	nafnbót
rather	heldur
Raudaberg (place)	Rauðabergi
read	lesit
realised	þykjast
reason	gegndi
received	tók
red	rauðum
released	lausan
remember	mundið
repay	launa
rest	hvílast
retainers	hirð
return	móti
returned	aptr

English	Old Icelandic
riders	ríða
riding	reiðingr, ríða
riding-clothes	reiðklæðum
rode	ríða
room	herbergi

S, s

English	Old Icelandic
said	kveðst, sagði, sagt, segist, segja, svarar
same-name	samnafna
Sámi (name)	Finna
sat	sat, situr
saw	sá, sért, Sjá
say	seg, segja
seats	sætis
seeking	leita
seen	séð
seldom	sjaldan
sends	sendi
sent	sendi, sendir, sent
separate	skilja
separated	skildum
serpent	Orminum
served	þjóna
set	settu
settled	bjó
shall	munum, skal, skulu
she	Hún
ship	skip, skipsins
ships	skips
ship's-prow	stafnana
shone	glóaði
short	skamma
short-distance	skammt
shortly	skjótliga, skjótt
should	mundi, skulum
should-be	væri
showed	sýndi
signed	signa
silver	silfri
since	síðan
skilled-in-magic	fjölkunnigr
so	á, Sú, svo
some	nokkurt, sumt

Word List (English to Old Icelandic)

English	Old Icelandic
son	niður, sonur
sons	syni
south	suður
splendid	skrautligri
spoke	kvað, mæla, mælti, tala
sports	íþróttir
stand	standa, Stöndum
staved	stafat
stepped	stigu
stood	standa, stóð
stop	stöðva
straight-away	þegar
strange	undr
such	slík
summer	sumri
surpassed	bar, yfirstigna
surplus	aflat

T, t

English	Old Icelandic
tables	borð
take	taka
taken	tekin
tent	tjald, tjaldi
than	en
thane	þegn
thanked	þakkaði
that	að, en, er, það, þeim, þetta
that-which	sem
the	að, hina, í, inni, inum, það, þann, þeir
the-bay	Víkinni
the-bishop	byskup
the-brothers	bræðrum
the-dragon's-neck	drekahálsinum
the-drinks	drykkinum
the-floor	gólfinu
the-forest	skóginn, skóginum
the-Grims (name)	Grímar, Grímum
the-Grims' (name)	Grímar
the-guests	Gestir
the-hall	höllina
the-horns	hornin, hornunum
theirs	síns, sínum, þeirra
the-king	konung, konungi, konungs, konungur
the-king's	konungs
the-last-time	næstunni
them	sért, þá, þau, þeim
themselves	sig
then	En, Er, Síðan, Þá, þeim
the-nature	náttúru
the-other	öðru
the-pole	stöngin
there	það
there-are	Eru
therefore	því
the-room	stofunni
the-same	sama
these	þær, þenna
the-sea	sjó
the-ship	skipinu
the-table	borða, borðum
the-woman	kona
they	Þær, þau, þeim, þeir, þeirra, þenna, Þetta
they-are	eru
things	þykkju
thinks	þótti
this	Þess, þessa, Þessi, þessu, þetta
Thori (name)	Þóri
Thorir (name)	Þórir
Thorstein (name)	Þorsteinn
those	þau
though	þó
thought	hugr, þótt, þótti, þóttist, þykir
three	þrír, þrjá, þrjár
threw	slógu
thriving	þrifligir
through	úr
time	stund
tired	þreyta
to	á, að, í, til, við
to-become	verða
together	saman, samt
to-give	gefi

Word List (English to Old Icelandic)

English	Old Icelandic	English	Old Icelandic
to-him	honum	*well*	velkominn
to-lay	liggja	*well-enough*	sæmiliga
told	sagði, svarar	*went*	ganga, Gengu, gengur
took	taka, tekur, tóku	*were*	er, hvar, væri, var, verða, voru
to-save	bjarga		
to-say	segja	*what*	hvað, hvar
to-you	þér, yður	*when*	er, nær
trade	kaupferð, kaups	*where*	er, hvar
trading-voyage	kaupferð	*which*	er
travel	fara, fer	*while*	meðan, stund
travelled	færðu, færum, fara, farið, fer, fór, fórtu, fóru	*who*	er
		why	Hví
treasures	gripir	*widely*	víða
twelve	tólf	*will*	vil
two	tvá, tveir, tvö	*willed*	vilduð
		winter	vetur, veturinn
		wish	vil

U, u

		wished	vildi, vildu, vilt
		with	með, sinni, við
uncertain	óvíst	*without*	nema
under	undir	*woman*	konu
until	til	*women*	konur, konurnar
up	upp	*words*	orðum
us	oss	*would*	mundu, vildi
use	nyt	*would-be*	væri

V, v

Y, y

various	ýmsum	*year*	ár
vessels	ker	*you*	þér, þú, yðar, yður
Vimund (name)	Vímund	*yours*	yðra, yðrar, yður
		you-to	þér
		Yule	jól, jóla

W, w

warrant	varða
was	en, er, væri, var, voru
was-named	heita, hét
way	veg
we	vér, við
wealth	fé, fjár
we-are	Erum
weather	veðrit, veður
welcomed	Fagna

A Word Comparison of Old Norse and Old Icelandic Words

Old Norse	Old Icelandic	English	Old Norse	Old Icelandic	English
áðr	áður	before	kveldit	kveldið	evening
allgóðr	allgóður	all-good	lætr	lætur	had
annarr	annar	another	líðr	líður	passed
annarr	annar	one	líðr	líður	passes
at	að	at	maðr	maður	a-man
at	að	in	maðr	maður	man
at	að	of	mik	mig	me
at	að	that	mikit	mikið	much
at	að	the	mjök	mjög	a-great
at	að	to	niðr	niður	down
betr	betur	better	niðr	niður	son
biðr	biður	asked	norðr	norður	north
bræðr	bræður	brothers	ok	og	also
eigi	ei	not	ok	og	and
eigi	ei	only	ór	úr	from
ek	eg	I	ór	úr	out-of
ekki	eigi	not	ór	úr	through
engu	öngu	not	orðit	orðið	become
færa	færi	brought	segir	svarar	said
farit	farið	travelled	segir	svarar	told
ferr	fer	travel	sér	sért	him
Ferr	fer	travelled	sér	sért	himself
fríðr	fríður	beautiful	sér	sért	saw
gefa	gefi	to-give	sér	sért	them
gengit	gengið	going	sét	séð	seen
gengr	gengur	went	síðr	síður	less
hafa	hafi	at-sea	sik	sig	themselves
hafa	hafi	had	sitr	situr	sat
heðan	héðan	hence	sonr	sonur	son
hefði	hefðu	had	spyrr	spyr	asked
heldr	heldur	rather	suðr	suður	south
helzt	helst	keep	svá	svo	so
hingat	hingað	here	svarar	svaraði	answered
hvárt	hvort	either	tekr	tekur	took
hvat	hvað	what	þangat	þangað	from-there
kemr	kemur	came	Þar	það	there
komit	komið	came	Þat	það	it
konungr	konungur	king	þat	það	it-was
Konungr	konungur	the-King	þat	það	that

A Word Comparison of Old Norse and Old Icelandic

Old Norse	Old Icelandic	English
þat	það	the
þeira	þeirra	theirs
þeira	þeirra	they
þykkir	þykir	thought
þykkjast	þykjast	realised
tvau	tvö	two
várr	vor	aware
várr	vor	ours
váru	voru	was
váru	voru	were
veðr	veður	weather
vel	velkominn	well
Verðr	Verður	became
verit	verið	been
vetr	vetur	winter
vetrinn	veturinn	winter
vill	vilt	wished
vit	við	we
vit	við	with
vita	viti	certainly
vita	viti	know
yðr	yður	to-you
yðr	yður	you
yðr	yður	yours

www.ingramcontent.com/pod-product-compliance
Lightning Source LLC
Chambersburg PA
CBHW051424070526
44584CB00023B/3563